What's the Best Movie Trivia Book?

2,000 Questions Across 9 Decades

David Fickes

Introduction

What you find in most trivia is a lot of erroneous or outdated information or questions that are so simple or esoteric that they aren't interesting. It is difficult to come up with interesting questions that are at the right level of difficulty that a wide variety of people can enjoy them, and they are something that you feel you should know or want to know. I have tried to ensure that the information is as accurate as possible, and to retain its accuracy, I have also tried to avoid questions whose answers can easily change with time.

Movie trivia is fun because it brings back so many memories; you can often see the answers visually in your mind. There are 2,000 questions in 10 categories arranged by decades from the 1930s to the 2010s plus an all-time category. To make it quick and easy to test yourself or others without initially seeing the answers, each category is divided into short quizzes with 10 questions followed by their answers.

If you enjoyed this book and learned a little and would like others to enjoy it also, please put out a review or rating. If you scan the QR code below, it will take you directly to the Amazon review and rating page.

Contents

All-Time

Quiz 1

1) Who was the first African American actress to win the Best Actress Oscar?
2) Sterling Holloway was the original voice of what Disney character?
3) What film has the first appearance of Mickey Mouse in a Disney animated feature?
4) What woman has the most Oscar nominations?
5) For what movie did Elizabeth Taylor win her first Oscar?
6) Who has the longest screen time performance to ever win the Best Actor Oscar?
7) What was the only film personally produced by Walt Disney to be nominated for the Best Picture Oscar?
8) What are the names of the five Marx brothers?
9) What is the only Charlie Chaplin film nominated for a Best Picture Oscar?
10) Who was the first Australian born actor to win an Oscar?

Quiz 1 Answers

1) Halle Berry – *Monster's Ball* (2001)
2) Winnie the Pooh
3) *Fantasia* – 1940
4) Edith Head – 35 for costume design
5) *BUtterfield 8* – 1960
6) Charlton Heston – 2 hours 1 minute and 23 seconds for *Ben-Hur* (1959)
7) *Mary Poppins* – 1964
8) Groucho, Chico, Harpo, Zeppo, Gummo
9) *The Great Dictator* – 1940
10) Geoffrey Rush – *Shine* in 1996

Quiz 2

1) What was the first science fiction film to win the Best Picture Oscar?
2) How many actors or actresses have received Oscar nominations for playing the same character twice?
3) In movie making, what job does the gaffer do?

4) Adjusted for inflation, what is the highest grossing western of all time in the U.S.?
5) What is the only G-rated movie to win the Best Picture Oscar?
6) What was the first independent film nominated for the Best Picture Oscar?
7) What two actresses share the record with five consecutive Best Actress Oscar nominations?
8) Who is the only actor to appear in multiple films and have every one nominated for the Best Picture Oscar?
9) The "no animals were harmed" statement on movies only applies when?
10) What is the highest grossing foreign language or subtitled film ever in the U.S.?

Quiz 2 Answers

1) *The Shape of Water* (2017)
2) Six – Sylvester Stallone (Rocky Balboa), Paul Newman (Fast Eddie Felson), Cate Blanchett (Queen Elizabeth I), Al Pacino (Michael Corleone), Peter O'Toole (King Henry II), Bing Crosby (Father O'Malley)
3) Chief electrician
4) *Butch Cassidy and the Sundance Kid* – 1969
5) *Oliver!* - 1968
6) *Kiss of the Spider Woman* – 1985
7) Bette Davis (1938-1942) and Greer Garson (1941-1945)
8) John Cazale – He appeared in *The Godfather*, *The Conversation*, *The Godfather Part II*, *Dog Day Afternoon*, and *The Deer Hunter*.
9) While film is recording
10) *The Passion of the Christ* – 2004

Quiz 3

1) Who has the shortest screen time performance to ever win an acting Oscar?
2) For what movie did Gene Kelly receive his only acting Oscar nomination?
3) What was the first commercial film to be shown in stereophonic sound?
4) After dropping out 34 years earlier, Steven Spielberg got his Bachelor of Arts degree from Cal State Long Beach; what did he submit for credit for his final project in advanced film making?

5) Who is the only actor or actress to win a best supporting Oscar two years in a row?
6) What was Judy Garland's real name?
7) Who has won the most Best Supporting Actor or Actress Oscars?
8) What is the highest grossing romantic comedy of all time in the U.S.?
9) What film series has the most Oscar nominations?
10) What character has been portrayed by Reginald Owen, Alistair Sim, and Albert Finney?

Quiz 3 Answers

1) Beatrice Straight – 5 minutes and 2 seconds for *Network* (1976)
2) *Anchors Aweigh* (1946)
3) *Fantasia* – 1940
4) *Schindler's List*
5) Jason Robards for *All the President's Men* (1976) and *Julia* (1977)
6) Frances Gumm
7) Walter Brennan – three for *Come and Get It* (1936), *Kentucky* (1938), *The Westerner* (1940)
8) *My Big Fat Greek Wedding*
9) *Lord of the Rings* trilogy – 30 nominations
10) Ebenezer Scrooge

Quiz 4

1) What was the word's first computer animated feature film?
2) Who was the first non-British act to perform a James Bond movie theme song?
3) What is the only movie character that has won Oscars for two different actors?
4) What person has the most Oscar nominations?
5) Who is the only Oscar winner whose parents were both Oscar winners?
6) What actor has appeared in the largest number of Best Picture Oscar winning movies?
7) What is the only X-rated movie to win the Best Picture Oscar?
8) What are the only three films to win all five major Academy Awards (best picture, director, actor, actress, screenplay)?
9) Who is the oldest Best Actress Oscar winner?
10) For what film did John Wayne win his only Oscar?

Quiz 4 Answers

1) *Toy Story* – 1995
2) Nancy Sinatra - *You Only Live Twice*
3) Vito Corleone – Marlon Brando in *The Godfather* and Robert de Niro in *The Godfather Part II*
4) Walt Disney – 59
5) Liza Minnelli
6) Franklyn Farnum – He was a character actor in 433 films including seven best picture winners – *The Life of Emile Zola* (1937), *Going My Way* (1944), *The Lost Weekend* (1945), *Gentleman's Agreement* (1947), *All About Eve* (1950), *The Greatest Show on Earth* (1952), and *Around the World in 80 Days* (1956).
7) *Midnight Cowboy* – It was X-rated at the time of the award; in 1971, its rating was changed to R.
8) *It Happened One Night* (1934), *One Flew Over the Cuckoo's Nest* (1975), *The Silence of the Lambs* (1991)
9) Jessica Tandy – 80 years old for *Driving Miss Daisy* (1989)
10) *True Grit* – 1969

Quiz 5

1) Who played sidekick to Hopalong Cassidy, Gene Autry, Roy Rogers, and John Wayne?
2) Who is the youngest Best Actress Oscar winner?
3) Who was the first actor to win the Best Actor Oscar for a musical performance?
4) What was Kirk Douglas' film debut?
5) What was the first film with sound to win the Best Picture Oscar?
6) What judge did Walter Brennan, Edgar Buchanan, and Paul Newman all portray?
7) What film star was the first to appear on a postage stamp?
8) What was the screen name of Edda Van Heemstra?
9) Who appeared in more than 30 Alfred Hitchcock films?
10) What was the first science fiction movie nominated for the Best Picture Oscar?

Quiz 5 Answers

1) Gabby Hayes
2) Marlee Matlin – 21 years old for *Children of a Lesser God* (1986)

4

3) James Cagney – *Yankee Doodle Dandy* in 1942
4) *The Strange Love of Martha Ivers* – 1946
5) *The Broadway Melody* – 1929
6) Roy Bean
7) Grace Kelly
8) Audrey Hepburn
9) Alfred Hitchcock
10) *A Clockwork Orange* (1971)

Quiz 6

1) What musical film has won the most Oscars?
2) Who are the only brother and sister to win acting Oscars?
3) What movie introduced the song that would become Walt Disney's theme song?
4) In what Alfred Hitchcock film does he make his usual appearance in a newspaper weight loss ad?
5) How many movies did Spencer Tracy and Katharine Hepburn make together?
6) In what movie did Clint Eastwood have his first credited acting role?
7) What Best Picture Oscar winning film has the longest title?
8) What was the last movie to feature Katharine Hepburn and Spencer Tracy?
9) What film had a 20-year gap between its release and winning an Oscar?
10) The first Cannes Film Festival was called off after screening only one film; why?

Quiz 6 Answers

1) *Gigi* (1958) – It won nine Oscars which is surpassed only by *Ben-Hur*, *Titanic*, and *The Lord of the Rings: The Return of the King*.
2) Lionel and Ethel Barrymore
3) *Pinocchio* – "When You Wish Upon a Star" in 1940
4) *Lifeboat* – Due to the setting in a lifeboat, he couldn't make his usual in person cameo appearance.
5) Nine – *Woman of the Year* (1942), *Keeper of the Flame* (1943), *Without Love* (1945), *The Sea of Grass* (1947), *State of the Union* (1948), *Adam's Rib* (1949), *Pat and Mike* (1952), *Desk Set* (1957), *Guess Who's Coming to Dinner* (1967)
6) *Francis in the Navy* (1955) - with Donald O'Connor and Francis the Talking Mule

7) *The Lord of the Rings: The Return of the King* – 2003
8) *Guess Who's Coming to Dinner* – 1967
9) *Limelight* – It was officially released in 1952 but was not released in Los Angeles County and eligible for an Oscar until 1972. It won a Best Original Score Oscar in 1973 and is Charlie Chaplin's only competitive Oscar win.
10) WWII broke out.

Quiz 7

1) For what film did the first woman win a Best Animated Feature Oscar?
2) Who played Tarzan in more movies than anyone else?
3) What is the only Walt Disney animated feature film that runs for two hours or more?
4) Who is the only author to have his works simultaneously number one in television, film, and books?
5) For what movie did Tony Curtis receive his only Best Actor Oscar nomination?
6) Directed by Gene Kelly, what was the last film starring James Stewart and Henry Fonda?
7) Who is the only person nominated for Oscars for acting, writing, producing, and directing the same film?
8) What are the only two Best Picture Oscar winning films that were based on best musical Tony Award winners?
9) What movie sold the most tickets all time in the U.S.?
10) Morgan Freeman has been in multiple Best Picture Oscar winning films; what is the only one where he also won an acting Oscar?

Quiz 7 Answers

1) *Brave* (2012) – Brenda Chapman
2) Johnny Weissmuller – 12 films
3) *Fantasia* – 1940
4) Michael Crichton – *ER* (television), *Jurassic Park* (film), *Disclosure* (book)
5) *The Defiant Ones* – 1958
6) *The Cheyenne Social Club* – 1970
7) Warren Beatty – twice for *Heaven Can Wait* (1978) and *Reds* (1981)
8) *My Fair Lady* and *The Sound of Music*
9) *Gone with the Wind* – About 208 million tickets have been sold; the U.S. population in 1939 when it was released was 131 million.
10) *Million Dollar Baby* – 2004

Quiz 8

1) Michael Jackson wanted to buy Marvel Comics; what was his primary motive?
2) What is the only film ever to have only one Oscar nomination in total and win Best Picture?
3) What real person has been portrayed most often in films?
4) What is the screen name of Archibald Leach?
5) What is the only film Henry Fonda and Jane Fonda made together?
6) Two films share the record for most Oscar nominations without any wins at 11; what are they?
7) The term blockbuster has meanings going back to large bombs in WWII, but as it is used to describe films, what was the first movie that the term was really applied to?
8) What is the highest grossing hand drawn animated film in history?
9) What year's Oscar ceremony saw the unusual occurrence where the real-life people whose lives were portrayed in the Best Actor and Best Actress Oscar winning performances were both in attendance?
10) What was the first film by the Marx Brothers?

Quiz 8 Answers

1) He wanted to play Spider Man in his own movie.
2) *Grand Hotel* – 1932
3) Napoleon Bonaparte
4) Cary Grant
5) *On Golden Pond* – 1981
6) *The Turning Point* (1977), *The Color Purple* (1985)
7) *Jaws* – 1975
8) *The Lion King*
9) 1981 – Sissy Spacek won Best Actress for her portrayal of Loretta Lynn in *Coal Miner's Daughter*, and Robert De Niro won for his portrayal of Jake LaMotta in *Raging Bull*. Both Loretta Lynn and Jake Lamotta were in attendance.
10) *The Cocoanuts* – 1929

Quiz 9

1) What movie features Jean Arthur's only Oscar nominated performance?
2) What is George C. Scott's middle name?
3) What was Spencer Tracy's last film?

4) What was the first animated film nominated for the Best Picture Oscar?
5) Adjusted for inflation, what is the highest grossing animated movie of all time in the U.S.?
6) Who has the most acting Oscar nominations?
7) For what film did Frank Sinatra win his only acting Oscar?
8) What was the first movie DVD sent out by Netflix in 1998?
9) What Oscar winning film is based on a novel by an American Civil War general who was also governor of the New Mexico Territory?
10) Adjusted for inflation, what is the highest grossing R-rated movie of all time in the U.S.?

Quiz 9 Answers

1) *The More the Merrier* – with Joel McCrea and Charles Coburn in 1943
2) Campbell
3) *Guess Who's Coming to Dinner*
4) *Beauty and the Beast* – 1991
5) *Snow White and the Seven Dwarfs* – 1937
6) Meryl Streep
7) *From Here to Eternity* - 1953
8) *Beetlejuice*
9) *Ben-Hur* – Lew Wallace published *Ben-Hur: A Tale of the Christ* in 1880; it was the all-time best-selling novel in the U.S. until the publication of *Gone with the Wind* in 1936. Wallace's novel was also the first work of fiction ever to be blessed by a pope.
10) *The Exorcist* – 1973

Quiz 10

1) What Oscar winning actress was the Connecticut state golf champion at age 16?
2) Who was the first actor to receive 10 Oscar acting nominations?
3) Adjusted for inflation, what is the all-time highest grossing movie in the U.S.?
4) What was Howard Hawks' first western film?
5) What was Burt Lancaster's film debut?
6) What was the world's first X-rated cartoon?
7) What movie won Cher her only Oscar?
8) Who is the only person with four acting Oscars?
9) Who is the oldest Oscar acting nominee in any category?

10) Adjusted for inflation, what is the earliest movie made that has grossed $1 billion in the U.S.?

Quiz 10 Answers

1) Katharine Hepburn
2) Laurence Olivier – 1978
3) *Gone with the Wind* – followed by *Star Wars, The Sound of Music, E.T. the Extra-Terrestrial, Titanic*
4) *Red River* – 1948 with John Wayne and Montgomery Clift
5) *The Killers* – 1946
6) *Fritz the Cat* – 1972
7) *Moonstruck* – 1987
8) Katharine Hepburn
9) Christopher Plummer – 88 years old for *All the Money in the World* (2017)
10) *Snow White and the Seven Dwarfs* – 1937

Quiz 11

1) For what movie did the first woman win a Best Picture Oscar?
2) For what film did Audrey Hepburn win her only Oscar?
3) What was the first animated Disney film to have an interracial romance?
4) What is the only Best Picture Oscar winning film starring Gregory Peck?
5) Who was the first African American to win the Best Supporting Actor Oscar?
6) What was the first film to win at least 10 Academy Awards?
7) For what film was the first posthumous Oscar of any kind awarded?
8) Anthony Daniels plays what character in a series of films?
9) What movie has the highest number of on-screen deaths of all time?
10) What individual has won the most Oscars?

Quiz 11 Answers

1) *The Sting* – 1973
2) *Roman Holiday* - 1953
3) *Pocahontas* – 1995
4) *Gentleman's Agreement* – 1947
5) Louis Gossett Jr. – *An Officer and a Gentleman* (1982)
6) *Ben-Hur* – 1959

7) *Gone with the Wind* – screenwriter Sidney Howard
8) C-3PO - *Star Wars*
9) *The Lord of the Rings: The Return of the King* – 836 deaths
10) Walt Disney – 22 competitive and 4 honorary awards

Quiz 12

1) For what film did George Burns win his only Oscar?
2) Who is the oldest Best Actor Oscar winner?
3) What was the first movie to make $100 million at the box office?
4) What movie has the record for the largest Oscar sweep – winning every category it was nominated for?
5) What is the only Best Picture Oscar winner with a hyphen in its title?
6) What was the first sequel nominated for a Best Picture Oscar?
7) Who was the first actress to star in three films nominated for the Best Picture Oscar in the same year?
8) Who is the youngest actor ever nominated for an Oscar?
9) What actor has been portrayed most on the screen by other actors?
10) Adjusted for inflation, what was the first film to surpass the budget for *Cleopatra* in 1963?

Quiz 12 Answers

1) *The Sunshine Boys* (1975) – best supporting actor
2) Anthony Hopkins – 83 years old for *The Father* (2020)
3) *Jaws* - 1975
4) *The Lord of the Rings: Return of the King* – It won all 11 Oscars it was nominated for.
5) *Ben-Hur*
6) *The Bells of St. Mary's* (1945)– sequel to *Going My Way* (1944)
7) Claudette Colbert – *Cleopatra*, *Imitation of Life*, and *It Happened One Night* in 1935
8) Justin Henry – eight years old for *Kramer vs. Kramer* (1979)
9) Charlie Chaplin
10) *Waterworld* – 1995

Quiz 13

1) What was the first animated film to win a competitive category Oscar?
2) Only two Best Picture Oscar winners have received acting nominations in all four categories; what are the two movies?

3) What was the debut film for Gene Wilder?

4) What was the screen name of Lee Yuen Kam?

5) What are the only two films with co-directors to win the Best Director Oscar?

6) Who directed *Dr. Strangelove or: How I Learned to Stop Worrying and Love the Bomb* and *2001: A Space Odyssey*?

7) Who is the oldest winner of a supporting acting Oscar?

8) What film was Leslie Caron's debut?

9) What was the only film directed by Orson Welles to show a profit in its original release?

10) What was the last film John F. Kennedy saw before his assassination?

Quiz 13 Answers

1) *Pinocchio* (1940) - Two years earlier *Snow White and the Seven Dwarfs* had won a special Oscar.

2) *Mrs. Miniver* (1942) and *From Here to Eternity* (1953)

3) *Bonnie and Clyde* – 1967

4) Bruce Lee

5) *West Side Story* with Robert Wise and Jerome Robbins in 1961 and *No Country for Old Men* with Joel and Ethan Coen in 2007

6) Stanley Kubrick

7) Christopher Plummer – 82 years old for best supporting actor in *Beginners* (2011)

8) *An American in Paris* (1951) – She was 19 at the time when she starred with Gene Kelly.

9) *The Stranger* – 1946

10) *Tom Jones* – 1963

Quiz 14

1) How many films did Humphrey Bogart and Lauren Bacall make together?

2) What was the first movie to gross $2 billion worldwide?

3) For what film did Fred Astaire receive his only acting Oscar nomination?

4) Who is the only person to write back to back Best Picture Oscar winners?

5) Prior to *The Artist* in 2011, what was the last entirely black and white movie to win the Best Picture Oscar?

6) After *Sleeping Beauty* in 1959, what was the next fairy tale produced by

Disney?

7) Two films share the record for most Oscars by a foreign film at four each; what are the movies?

8) Who are the only two people to win posthumous acting Oscars?

9) For which movie did James Stewart win his only Best Actor Oscar?

10) What was the first horror film nominated for the Best Picture Oscar?

Quiz 14 Answers

1) Four – *To Have and Have Not* (1944), *The Big Sleep* (1946), *Dark Passage* (1947), *Key Largo* (1948)

2) *Avatar* – 2009

3) *The Towering Inferno* - 1975

4) Paul Haggis – *Million Dollar Baby* and *Crash*

5) *The Apartment* (1960) – *Schindler's List* in 1993 had color in some scenes.

6) *The Little Mermaid* – 1989

7) *Fanny and Alexander* (1982) and *Crouching Tiger, Hidden Dragon* (2000)

8) Peter Finch in 1976 for *Network* and Heath Ledger in 2008 for *The Dark Knight*

9) *The Philadelphia Story* – 1940

10) *The Exorcist* – 1973

Quiz 15

1) What was Vincent Price's last film?

2) What was the first R-rated movie to win the Best Picture Oscar?

3) Who is the youngest Best Actor Oscar nominee?

4) Only three Christmas movies have been nominated for the Best Picture Oscar; what are they?

5) What is the longest movie to ever win the Best Picture Oscar?

6) Who is the oldest Best Director Oscar winner?

7) For what film did James Cagney win his only Oscar?

8) Who is the only performer nominated for two Oscars for the same performance?

9) What classic film originated from a Christmas card?

10) In the James Bond films, what does the acronym SPECTRE stand for?

Quiz 15 Answers

1) *Edward Scissorhands* – 1990

2) *The French Connection* - 1971

3) Jackie Cooper – 9 years old for *Skippy* (1931)
4) *It's a Wonderful Life* (1946), *Miracle on 34th Street* (1947), *The Bishop's Wife* (1947)
5) *Gone with the Wind* - 238 minutes
6) Clint Eastwood – 74 years old for *Million Dollar Baby* (2005)
7) *Yankee Doodle Dandy*
8) Barry Fitzgerald – He was nominated for Best Actor and Best Supporting Actor for *Going My Way* (1944); current Academy rules don't allow this to happen.
9) *It's a Wonderful Life* – Philip Van Doren Stern had written a short story, *The Greatest Gift*, and had unsuccessfully tried to get it published. He sent it out as a 21-page Christmas card to his closest friends; a producer at RKO Pictures got hold of it and purchased the movie rights.
10) Special Executive for Counterintelligence Terror Revenge and Extortion

Quiz 16

1) What was Alfred Hitchcock's only Best Picture Oscar winner?
2) What was the first full length color cartoon talking picture?
3) What actor has the most Oscar nominations without a win?
4) Who has won the most Best Director Oscars?
5) What actor played Wyatt Earp, Frank James, and Abraham Lincoln?
6) Vincente Minnelli met and directed his future wife Judy Garland during the filming of what movie?
7) Who was the first film star to earn $1 million for a single film?
8) Peter Sellers, Alan Arkin, Roger Moore, Roberto Benigni, and Steve Martin have all played what character?
9) What is the shortest film to win a Best Picture Oscar?
10) What was the first non-documentary film given permission to film in Mecca?

Quiz 16 Answers

1) *Rebecca* – 1940
2) *Snow White and the Seven Dwarfs*
3) Peter O'Toole – eight
4) John Ford - four
5) Henry Fonda
6) *Meet Me in St. Louis* - 1944
7) Elizabeth Taylor – *Cleopatra* in 1963

8) Inspector Clouseau – Pink Panther movies
9) *Marty* (1955) – 90 minutes
10) *Malcolm X* – 1992

Quiz 17

1) Adjusted for inflation, what is the only horror film to gross $1 billion in the U.S.?
2) What is the only Hollywood film to make the Vatican's approved list in the religious category?
3) What movie holds the record for most Oscar nominations for a foreign film?
4) What was the first Disney animated feature film set in America?
5) Who is the only person with a star in each of the five categories (movies, television, music, radio, live performance) on the Hollywood Walk of Fame?
6) For what movie did Marlon Brando win his first Oscar?
7) Who is the only person to win Oscars for Best Actress and Best Song?
8) Who was the first actress to receive 10 Oscar acting nominations?
9) Who has the longest screen time performance to win a supporting actor or actress Oscar?
10) Shirley Bassey sang the theme song for which three James Bond films?

Quiz 17 Answers

1) *The Exorcist* – 1973
2) *Ben-Hur*
3) *Crouching Tiger, Hidden Dragon* – 10 nominations, 4 wins
4) *Dumbo*
5) Gene Autry
6) *On the Waterfront* – 1954
7) Barbra Streisand – Best Actress Oscar for *Funny Girl* (1968) and Best Original Song Oscar for "Evergreen" from *A Star is Born* (1976)
8) Bette Davis – 1962
9) Tatum O'Neal – 1 hour, 6 minutes and 58 seconds for *Paper Moon* (1973)
10) *Goldfinger, Diamonds Are Forever, Moonraker*

Quiz 18

1) Marnie Nixon did what for Deborah Kerr, Natalie Wood, and Audrey

Hepburn?

2) Who was the first actor to appear on the cover of *Time* magazine?

3) What movie earned Clint Eastwood his first Best Director Oscar?

4) What are the only two Pulitzer Prize winning novels made into Best Picture Oscar winners?

5) What is Richard Gere's middle name?

6) Who is the actress sister of Olivia de Havilland?

7) How many movies did Gene Wilder and Richard Pryor co-star in?

8) What country made the world's first feature film in 1906?

9) What is the only full musical film to win a Best Original Screenplay Oscar?

10) For what film did Sidney Poitier win a Best Actor Oscar?

Quiz 18 Answers

1) She dubbed their singing voices.

2) Charlie Chaplin

3) *Unforgiven*

4) *Gone with the Wind* and *All the King's Men*

5) Tiffany

6) Joan Fontaine

7) Four – *Silver Streak* (1976), *Stir Crazy* (1980), *See No Evil, Hear No Evil* (1989), *Another You* (1991)

8) Australia

9) *An American in Paris* (1951)

10) *Lilies of the Field*

Quiz 19

1) Who are the only two actors who have won consecutive Best Actor Oscars?

2) What three John Wayne films have "Rio" in the title?

3) What is the only remake of a regular television series to be nominated for a Best Picture Oscar?

4) Only four films have received two Best Actress Oscar nominations; what are they?

5) What was the first foreign film to win the Best Picture Oscar?

6) Humphrey Bogart starred in the first film John Huston directed; what was it?

7) What two families have three generations of Oscar winners?

8) What is the best-selling movie soundtrack of all time?

9) Who are the only sisters to win acting Oscars?

10) With nine wins, what film holds the British Academy Awards (BAFTAs) record?

Quiz 19 Answers

1) Spencer Tracy for *Captains Courageous* (1937) and *Boys Town* (1938) and Tom Hanks for *Philadelphia* (1993) and *Forrest Gump* (1994)

2) *Rio Grande* (1950), *Rio Bravo* (1959), *Rio Lobo* (1970)

3) *The Fugitive* (1993) – Oscar winner *Marty* (1955) was a remake of a television movie; Oscar nominated *Traffic* (2000) was adapted from a miniseries.

4) *All About Eve* (Anne Baxter and Bette Davis), *Suddenly Last Summer* (Katharine Hepburn and Elizabeth Taylor), *Terms of Endearment* (Shirley MacLaine and Debra Winger), *Thelma & Louise* (Geena Davis and Susan Sarandon)

5) *Hamlet* (1948) – from Great Britain

6) *The Maltese Falcon*

7) Huston (Walter, John, and Anjelica) and Coppola (Carmine, Francis Ford, and Sofia)

8) *The Bodyguard*

9) Olivia de Haviland and Joan Fontaine

10) *Butch Cassidy and the Sundance Kid* – 1969

Quiz 20

1) What cartoon duo won seven Oscars for best animated short film?

2) What are the only two films to win Best Picture, Director and Screenplay at the Golden Globes, BAFTAs and the Oscars?

3) Who was the first person to win directing, writing, and best picture Oscars for the same film?

4) Who was the first actor or actress to win a competitive acting Oscar for a Walt Disney film?

5) What international movie star was born in a bombed out French village during WWI?

6) David Niven has the record for the shortest screen time performance to ever win the Best Actor Oscar; what film was it in?

7) Who is the oldest Best Actor Oscar nominee?

8) Adjusted for inflation, what is the highest grossing comedy of all time in the U.S.?

9) What is the only film directed by John Ford to win the Best Picture Oscar?

10) For what film did Steven Spielberg win his first Oscar?

Quiz 20 Answers

1) Tom and Jerry
2) *Schindler's List* (1993) and *Slumdog Millionaire* (2008)
3) Billy Wilder - *The Apartment* in 1960
4) Julie Andrews – *Mary Poppins* (1964)
5) Rin Tin Tin
6) *Separate Tables* (1958)– Niven was on screen for 23 minutes and 39 seconds.
7) Richard Farnsworth – 79 years old for *The Straight Story* (1999)
8) *Home Alone* – 1990
9) *How Green Was My Valley* – 1941
10) *Schindler's List*

Quiz 21

1) Who was the first actor to receive a posthumous Oscar nomination?
2) What Best Picture Oscar nominee used the "F" word the most times?
3) What actor has died the most times on screen?
4) What country makes the most films per year?
5) Who said during their one and only Oscar acceptance speech, "I think they gave it to me because I'm the oldest"?
6) Who is the only person named Oscar to win an Oscar?
7) What country has won the Best Foreign Language Film Oscar the most times?
8) What is the only movie to ever have three Best Actor Oscar nominations?
9) What was the first movie from a non-English speaking country to win the Best Picture Oscar?
10) What was the third western ever to win the Best Picture Oscar?

Quiz 21 Answers

1) James Dean – *East of Eden* in 1956
2) *The Wolf of Wall Street* – more than 500 times
3) John Hurt – 43 times including *Alien*, *Spaceballs*, *V for Vendetta*, *Hellboy*
4) India

5) Jessica Tandy – 80 years old at the time
6) Oscar Hammerstein II
7) Italy
8) *Mutiny on the Bounty* – Clark Gable, Charles Laughton, and Franchot Tone in 1936
9) *The Artist* – from France in 2011
10) *Unforgiven* (1992) – preceded by *Cimarron* (1931) and *Dances with Wolves* (1990)

Quiz 22

1) Who is Melanie Griffith's mother?
2) What was Walt Disney's first animated feature film?
3) What was Disney's first live action feature movie?
4) What was the first full length feature film based on a television series?
5) Who is the first person to win an acting Oscar for portraying a real acting Oscar winner?
6) What Walt Disney film has the most Oscar wins with five?
7) What was the first Pixar film to win the Best Animated Feature Oscar?
8) What woman has won the most Oscars?
9) French novelist Pierre Boulle is best known for two novels that were both made into movies; one is *The Bridge Over the River Kwai*; what is the other novel that was also made into a famous movie?
10) What movie was the film debut of Agnes Moorehead?

Quiz 22 Answers

1) Tippi Hedren – star of Alfred Hitchcock's *The Birds*
2) *Snow White and the Seven Dwarfs* – 1937
3) *Treasure Island* – 1950
4) *Dragnet* (1954) – starring Jack Webb
5) Cate Blanchett – Best Supporting Actress Oscar for portraying Katharine Hepburn in *The Aviator* (2004)
6) *Mary Poppins* – 1964
7) *Finding Nemo* – 2003
8) Edith Head – eight for costume design
9) *Planet of the Apes*
10) *Citizen Kane*

Quiz 23

1) Who is the only person to win an Olympic gold medal and an Oscar?
2) What is the only fantasy film to win the Best Picture Oscar?
3) What was the first western to win the Best Picture Oscar?
4) Who was the first actor or actress to reject their Oscar win?
5) What male actor has the most Oscar nominations?
6) Who is the youngest competitive Oscar winner ever?
7) What famous movie actor competed in the 1953 Mr. Universe bodybuilding competition?
8) For what film did Patty Duke win her only Oscar?
9) What film was Donna Reed's first starring role?
10) What film has won the most Oscars without winning best picture?

Quiz 23 Answers

1) Kobe Bryant – Olympic basketball gold medals in 2008 and 2012 and Best Animated Short Film for *Dear Basketball* in 2018
2) *The Lord of the Rings: The Return of the King* – 2003
3) *Cimarron* – 1931
4) George C. Scott – 1971 for *Patton*
5) Jack Nicholson
6) Tatum O'Neal – 10 years old for *Paper Moon* (1973)
7) Sean Connery
8) *The Miracle Worker* (1962) – She plays Helen Keller.
9) *It's a Wonderful Life* – 1946
10) *Cabaret* (1972) – eight Oscars

Quiz 24

1) What year did the first screen kiss between two men occur?
2) What was Charlie Chaplin's first talking picture?
3) How old was Shirley Temple when she made her last film?
4) What two films did Paul Newman play Fast Eddie Felson in?
5) What is the only film where the top two billed actors playing a married couple won the Best Actor and Best Actress Oscars?
6) Who is the youngest Best Actor Oscar winner?
7) Who was the first actress to win an Oscar for a performance entirely in a foreign language?
8) What was the first feature film broadcast on U.S. television?

9) Who is the only person to win the Best Actor Oscar three times?

10) Packy East, an amateur boxer, became famous as a comedian under what name?

Quiz 24 Answers

1) 1927 in *Wings* – It didn't cause any stir at the time.
2) *The Great Dictator* – 1940
3) 22
4) *The Hustler* and *The Color of Money*
5) *On Golden Pond* – 1981 with Henry Fonda and Katharine Hepburn
6) Adrien Brody – 29 years old for *The Pianist* (2002)
7) Sophia Loren – 1962 for *Two Women*
8) *The Wizard of Oz* – broadcast in 1956
9) Daniel Day-Lewis – *My Left Foot*, *There Will Be Blood*, *Lincoln*
10) Bob Hope

Quiz 25

1) What was the first Disney animated feature where the songs were not sung by the film's characters?
2) What three sports related movies have won the Best Picture Oscar?
3) What are the first names of the film making Coen brothers?
4) What is the only Best Picture Oscar nominated movie starring Barbara Stanwyck?
5) What is the only film where cartoon characters from Walt Disney and Warner Brothers appear together?
6) Who were the first father and son to win Oscars for the same film?
7) Why are Academy Awards called Oscars?
8) What three films are tied for the most Oscars at 11 each?
9) What actor is often credited with saving Warner Brothers Studio from bankruptcy and received the most votes for the Best Actor Oscar at the first Academy Awards in 1929 before being eliminated from the ballot?
10) What are the only two films to win three out of the four acting Oscars?

Quiz 25 Answers

1) *Bambi* – 1942
2) *Rocky*, *Chariots of Fire*, *Million Dollar Baby*
3) Joel and Ethan
4) *Double Indemnity* - 1944

5) *Who Framed Roger Rabbit* – 1988
6) Walter and John Huston – *The Treasure of the Sierra Madre*
7) Margaret Herrick, Academy librarian and future executive director, thought the statue looked like her uncle Oscar.
8) *Ben-Hur*, *Titanic*, *The Lord of the Rings: The Return of the King*
9) Rin Tin Tin – The Academy wanted to appear more serious and have a human win, so they removed him from the ballot and voted again.
10) *A Streetcar Named Desire* (1951) with Vivien Leigh, Karl Malden, and Kim Hunter and *Network* (1976) with Peter Finch, Faye Dunaway, and Beatrice Straight

Quiz 26

1) Who are the only five performers to win consecutive acting Oscars?
2) Three films share the record for most Oscar nominations with 14; what are the three movies?
3) What is the only Best Picture Oscar winner without any female speaking roles?
4) What was the first film released in the U.S. with the PG-13 rating?
5) Who built the world's first film studio?
6) Who is the first person born in the 21st century nominated for an acting Oscar?
7) What was the first film to win the Best Picture at the Academy Awards and BAFTAs and Best Picture – Musical or Comedy at the Golden Globe Awards?
8) Adjusted for inflation, what is the lowest grossing film to ever win the Best Picture Oscar?
9) What was the first Andrew Lloyd Webber musical made into a movie?
10) What is the only film based on a television show to win the Best Picture Oscar?

Quiz 26 Answers

1) Luise Rainer (1936 and 1937), Spencer Tracy (1937 and 1938), Katharine Hepburn (1967 and 1968), Jason Robards (1976 and 1977), Tom Hanks (1993 and 1994)
2) *All About Eve* (1950), *Titanic* (1997), *La La Land* (2016)
3) *Lawrence of Arabia* – 1962
4) *Red Dawn* (1984) – *Indiana Jones and the Temple of Doom* had been released three months earlier with a PG rating and caused an outcry which resulted in the new PG-13 rating option.

5) Thomas Edison
6) Quvenzhane Wallis – She was born in 2003 and was nominated for best actress for *Beasts of the Southern Wild* (2012).
7) *The Apartment* – 1960
8) *The Hurt Locker* – 2008
9) *Jesus Christ Superstar*
10) *Marty* – 1955

Quiz 27

1) Who is the only person to produce two consecutive Best Picture Oscar winners?
2) What was the first comedy to win the Best Picture Oscar?
3) What was Gregory Peck's film debut?
4) What was the first Disney animated feature set in present day at the time of its release?
5) What was the first completely digitally shot movie to win the Best Cinematography Oscar?
6) What was the first full color film to win the Best Picture Oscar?
7) What actor holds the record for the most years between Oscar nominations playing the same character?
8) What film holds the record for the longest time between the original and the sequel?
9) Who was voted most popular film performer in the U.S. in 1926?
10) What is the only movie Alfred Hitchcock made twice?

Quiz 27 Answers

1) David O. Selznick – *Gone with the Wind* (1939) and *Rebecca* (1940)
2) *It Happened One Night* – 1934
3) *Days of Glory* – 1944
4) *Dumbo* – 1941
5) *Avatar* – 2009
6) *Gone with the Wind*
7) Sylvester Stallone – 39 years between *Rocky* in 1976 and *Creed* in 2015
8) *Bambi* – *Bambi II* was released in 2006 which was 64 years after the original.
9) Rin Tin Tin
10) *The Man Who Knew Too Much* – 1934 and 1956

Quiz 28

1) What film has the most Oscar nominations without winning Best Picture?
2) What was the first U.S. film with a female director to gross over $100 million?
3) What film made Hattie McDaniel the first African American Oscar winner?
4) What year was *The Wizard of Oz* released?
5) What was the first sports film to win the Best Picture Oscar?
6) What actor or actress has the longest time between their first and last Oscars?
7) What was the very first film to win the Best Picture Oscar?
8) Katharine Hepburn never appeared in a film that won the Best Picture Oscar; what was the last film she appeared in that was nominated for the Best Picture Oscar?
9) What was the first talking motion picture with the sound in the film?
10) Who are the only two people to win both a Nobel Prize and an Oscar?

Quiz 28 Answers

1) *La La Land* – 14
2) *Big* – directed by Penny Marshall in 1988
3) *Gone with the Wind*
4) 1939
5) *Rocky* – 1976
6) Katharine Hepburn – 48 years from 1933 to 1981
7) *Wings* – 1927
8) *On Golden Pond* – 1981
9) *The Jazz Singer* – 1927
10) George Bernard Shaw won the Nobel Literature Prize in 1925 and the Best Adapted Screenplay Oscar for *Pygmalion* in 1936; Bob Dylan won the Best Original Song Oscar for "Things Have Changed" from *Wonder Boys* in 2000 and the Nobel Literature Prize in 2016.

Quiz 29

1) Who is the youngest Best Actress Oscar nominee?
2) Who are the only two actresses who have won consecutive Best Actress Oscars?
3) Four women have won the Best Actress Oscar for their debut acting

performance; who are they?

4) What film won Gregory Peck his second Best Actor Oscar?
5) Who was the first person to win an Oscar for acting and writing?
6) Who has the shortest screen time performance to ever win the Best Actress Oscar?
7) What movie holds the record for most weekends in the top 10 box office films in the U.S.?
8) What two films share the record for shortest film title for a Best Picture Oscar winner?
9) Who was the first actress to receive 20 Oscar acting nominations?
10) What was the first movie to gross $1 billion worldwide?

Quiz 29 Answers

1) Quvenzhane Wallis – 9 years old for *Beasts of the Southern Wild* (2012)
2) Luise Rainer for *The Great Ziegfeld* (1936) and *The Good Earth* (1937) and Katharine Hepburn for *Guess Who's Coming to Dinner* (1967) and *The Lion in Winter* (1968)
3) Shirley Booth for *Come Back, Little Sheba* (1952), Julie Andrews for *Mary Poppins* (1964), Barbra Streisand for *Funny Girl* (1968), Marlee Matlin for *Children of a Lesser God* (1986)
4) *To Kill a Mockingbird* - 1962
5) Emma Thompson – Best Actress Oscar for *Howards End* (1992) and Best Adapted Screenplay Oscar for *Sense and Sensibility* (1995)
6) Patricia Neal – 21 minutes and 51 seconds of screen time for *HUD* (1963)
7) *E.T. the Extra-Terrestrial* – 44 weekends
8) *Gigi* (1958) and *Argo* (2012)
9) Meryl Streep – 2016
10) *Titanic* – 1997

Quiz 30

1) What was the next film Orson Welles directed after *Citizen Kane*?
2) What was the first Disney animated film based on the life of a real person?
3) What movie did Dwight D. Eisenhower call "Simply the best film ever made. My number one favorite film"?
4) Who is the first protagonist in a Disney animated feature to have no dialogue?
5) What are the only two sequels to win Best Picture Oscars?

6) What film produced the first female Best Director Oscar?
7) Who was the first actress paid $20 million for a film?
8) Who are the only brothers to receive acting Oscar nominations?
9) What actor starred in both Alfred Hitchcock's *Rope* and *Strangers on a Train*?
10) Elvis Presley memorized every line from his all-time favorite movie; what was the film?

Quiz 30 Answers

1) *The Magnificent Ambersons* – 1942
2) *Pocahontas*
3) *The Big Country* (1958)
4) Dumbo – 1941
5) *The Godfather Part II* and *The Lord of the Rings: The Return of the King*
6) *The Hurt Locker* (2008)– Kathryn Bigelow
7) Julia Roberts – *Erin Brockovich* (2000)
8) River and Joaquin Phoenix
9) Farley Granger
10) *Patton*

Quiz 31

1) Who was the first actor to direct himself to a Best Actor Oscar?
2) What year did the NC-17 movie rating replace the X rating?
3) What was John Ford's first western with sound?
4) What science fiction movie was originally made in 1956 and remade in 1978 and 1993?
5) Who won the most Oscars in a single year?
6) The U.S. film industry relocated from New York to Los Angeles in large part because of what man?
7) Who is the oldest Best Actress Oscar nominee?
8) What was the first movie ever to gross $500 million worldwide in a single weekend?
9) Who has the longest screen time performance to ever win a Best Actress Oscar?
10) In accepting their Best Supporting Actor Oscar, who said, "Now I know there's a Santa Claus"?

Quiz 31 Answers

1) Laurence Olivier – *Hamlet* in 1948
2) 1990 – *Henry & June* was the first film to receive the Nc-17 rating.
3) *Stagecoach* – 1939
4) *Invasion of the Body Snatchers*
5) Walt Disney – four in 1953
6) Thomas Edison – He held many of the patents on the production and showing of movies and controlled the industry; film makers escaped to Los Angeles to get away from his control.
7) Emmanuelle Riva – 85 years old for *Amour* (2012)
8) *Jurassic World* – 2015
9) Vivien Leigh – 2 hours, 23 minutes and 32 seconds for *Gone with the Wind* (1939)
10) Edmund Gwenn – for his role as Santa Claus in *Miracle on 34th Street*

Quiz 32

1) What was the first film to win the Best Animated Feature Oscar?
2) For what film did Robert Redford win his only Oscar?
3) What was the first film Morgan Freeman provided narration for?
4) What actor holds the record with four consecutive Best Actor Oscar nominations?
5) What was the first film pairing Gene Wilder and Richard Pryor?
6) Who are the only two people to direct themselves to a best actor or best actress Oscar?
7) What movie holds the record for most consecutive weekends at number one in box office in the U.S.?
8) What was Cary Grant's last movie?
9) What major actor and director had their film debut in *Revenge of the Creature* in 1955?
10) Who is the first person to have the number one movie and record album in the same week?

Quiz 32 Answers

1) *Shrek* - 2001
2) Ordinary People (1980) – best director
3) *The Shawshank Redemption* - 1994
4) Marlon Brando (1951-1954)
5) *Silver Streak* – 1976

6) Laurence Olivier for *Hamlet* (1948) and Roberto Benigni for *Life Is Beautiful* (1997)
7) *Titanic* – 1997 for 15 weekends
8) *Walk Don't Run* – 1966
9) Clint Eastwood
10) Jennifer Lopez – 2001

1930s

Quiz 1

1) In *Captains Courageous*, who plays the boy picked up by the fishing boat?
2) Who plays Professor Higgins in *Pygmalion*?
3) Who plays the title role in *The Hunchback of Notre Dame*?
4) Who plays the title role in *Flash Gordon*?
5) For what movie did Katharine Hepburn win her first Best Actress Oscar?
6) Who plays the corrupt Senator Paine in *Mr. Smith Goes to Washington*?
7) What is the name of the island that is King Kong's home?
8) Who plays the title role in *My Man Godfrey*?
9) In Disney's *Snow White and the Seven Dwarfs*, what do the dwarfs mine?
10) Who plays the title role in *Scarface*?

Quiz 1 Answers

1) Freddie Bartholomew
2) Leslie Howard
3) Charles Laughton
4) Buster Crabbe
5) *Morning Glory* – 1933
6) Claude Rains
7) Skull Island
8) William Powell
9) Diamonds
10) Paul Muni

Quiz 2

1) What actor and actress play the young couple who want to get married in *You Can't Take It with You*?
2) What film features a wrongly convicted physician who is exiled to the Caribbean and becomes a pirate?
3) Who plays the sleuthing couple in the *Thin Man* series of films?
4) Who plays the divorcing couple in the comedy *The Awful Truth*?
5) Who plays the Wicked Witch of the West in *The Wizard of Oz*?
6) Who plays Captain Bligh in *Mutiny on the Bounty*?

7) What was the first movie Katharine Hepburn appeared in that was nominated for a Best Picture Oscar?
8) What was the filming location for *Stagecoach*?
9) What character does Groucho Marx play in *Duck Soup*?
10) In what movie did the Marx Brothers take on high society?

Quiz 2 Answers

1) James Stewart and Jean Arthur
2) *Captain Blood* – starring Errol Flynn
3) William Powell and Myrna Loy
4) Cary Grant and Irene Dunn
5) Margaret Hamilton
6) Charles Laughton
7) *Little Women* – her fourth film in 1933
8) Monument Valley, Arizona – John Ford used the location for eight more westerns.
9) Rufus T. Firefly
10) *A Night at the Opera*

Quiz 3

1) Who plays the title role in *The Hunchback of Notre Dame*?
2) What Katharine Hepburn movie is about a group of sisters growing up in 19th century America?
3) Who plays the wife of the title character in *Goodbye, Mr. Chips*?
4) In the Mark Twain classic story *Tom Sawyer*, who plays the title role?
5) What movie features Laurel and Hardy sneaking away to a lodge convention?
6) Who plays the patriarch of the eccentric family in *You Can't Take It with You*?
7) What is the name of Groucho Marx's character in *A Day at the Races*?
8) What instrument does the title character play in *Mr. Deeds Goes to Town*?
9) What is Dorothy's last name in *The Wizard of Oz*?
10) What film has the ending line "**Frankly, my dear, I don't give a damn**"?

Quiz 3 Answers

1) Charles Laughton
2) *Little Women*
3) Greer Garson

4) Jackie Coogan
5) *Sons of the Desert*
6) Lionel Barrymore
7) Dr. Hugo Z. Hackenbush
8) Tuba
9) Gale
10) *Gone with the Wind* – Clark Gable

Quiz 4

1) What comedy features Carole Lombard as Hazel Flagg who is misdiagnosed as being terminally ill?
2) Who plays Eliza Doolittle in *Pygmalion*?
3) Who plays the scarecrow in *The Wizard of Oz*?
4) A 1930 film was marketed as a documentary of a 1926 expedition led by British explorers Sir Hubert Winstead and Captain Daniel Swayne who found a Congo tribe that worshipped a giant gorilla. It turned out to be a total fake with Hollywood actors; Los Angeles children playing pygmies, etc., but it was still the 11th highest grossing film of the 1930s. What was the movie?
5) What role did Clark Gable play in *Mutiny on the Bounty*?
6) What two actors play the central characters George and Lennie in *Of Mice and Men*?
7) What is the name of the cult the British army is battling in *Gunga Din*?
8) In *Mr. Deeds Goes to Town*, what is the title character's first name?
9) What Alfred Hitchcock spy thriller features Robert Donat?
10) Who plays the title role in *Stella Dallas*?

Quiz 4 Answers

1) *Nothing Sacred*
2) Wendy Hiller
3) Ray Bolger
4) *Ingagi*
5) Fletcher Christian
6) Burgess Meredith and Lon Chaney Jr.
7) Thuggee
8) Longfellow
9) *The 39 Steps*
10) Barbara Stanwyck

Quiz 5

1) Robert Donat won a Best Actor Oscar for his portrayal of a character who ages 63 years in what film?
2) In *She Done Him Wrong*, Mae West says the famous line "Why don't you come up some time, and see me?"; what actor does she say it to?
3) John Wayne's first starring role was in what movie?
4) Who has the title role in *The Scarlet Pimpernel*?
5) What is the name of the dog owned by Nick and Nora Charles in *The Thin Man*?
6) Who plays the title role in *Dr. Jekyll and Mr. Hyde*?
7) Who plays Heathcliff in *Wuthering Heights*?
8) Who plays the title role in *Beau Geste*?
9) Who plays the cowardly lion in *The Wizard of Oz*?
10) What is the name of the tiny nation Groucho Marx rules in *Duck Soup*?

Quiz 5 Answers

1) *Goodbye, Mr. Chips*
2) Cary Grant
3) *The Big Trail* – 1930
4) Leslie Howard
5) Asta
6) Fredric March
7) Laurence Olivier
8) Gary Cooper
9) Bert Lahr
10) Freedonia

Quiz 6

1) Who plays Maid Marian in *The Adventures of Robin Hood*?
2) What character did Spencer Tracy play in a 1938 film that won him his second consecutive Best Actor Oscar?
3) Who plays the title role in *Bride of Frankenstein*?
4) Who plays the runaway heiress in *It Happened One Night*?
5) What was the first of 14 Sherlock Holmes films starring Basil Rathbone and Nigel Bruce?
6) "One morning I shot an elephant in my pajamas. How he got in my pajamas, I don't know," is a line from what movie?

7) What movie has the line "Oh, no, it wasn't the airplanes. It was beauty killed the beast"?

8) What was the number one U.S. box office film released in the 1930s?

9) Who received the only Oscar made of wood?

10) What film won Best Picture and Best Director Oscars and centers on the triumphs and tragedies of two English families from 1899 to 1933?

Quiz 6 Answers

1) Olivia de Havilland
2) Father Flanagan – *Boys Town*
3) Elsa Lanchester
4) Claudette Colbert
5) *The Hound of the Baskervilles*
6) *Animal Crackers* – Groucho Marx
7) *King Kong*
8) *Gone with the Wind* – Inflation adjusted, it is the all-time U.S. box office record holder.
9) Edgar Bergen and Charlie McCarthy
10) *Cavalcade*

Quiz 7

1) What was the first all color film nominated for the Best Picture Oscar?
2) Who directed *Stagecoach*?
3) What film has Bette Davis playing a young socialite dying from a brain tumor?
4) Who plays the American ambulance driver and the English nurse who fall in love during WWI in *A Farewell to Arms*?
5) How many Oscars did *Gone with the Wind* win?
6) What Hitchcock film deals with a missing governess on a train?
7) What film has Ronald Colman impersonating a foreign king?
8) For what film did Spencer Tracy win his first Best Actor Oscar?
9) What Mae West film features lines such as "When I'm good, I'm very good. But when I'm bad, I'm better," and "It's not the men in your life that counts, it's the life in your men"?
10) What Hitchcock film has a London detective on the trail of a bomber?

Quiz 7 Answers

1) *A Star is Born* – 1937

2) John Ford
3) *Dark Victory*
4) Gary Cooper and Helen Hayes
5) Nine
6) *The Lady Vanishes*
7) *The Prisoner of Zenda*
8) *Captains Courageous* – 1937
9) *I'm No Angel*
10) *Sabotage*

Quiz 8

1) In *Snow White and the Seven Dwarfs*, which of the dwarfs comes first alphabetically?
2) In *My Man Godfrey*, how does Carole Lombard's character meet Godfrey?
3) Who plays Little John in *The Adventures of Robin Hood*?
4) Who directed the screwball comedy *Bringing Up Baby*?
5) What Charlie Chaplin film has The Tramp trying to help a sightless flower girl?
6) What 1933 fantasy film has Cary Grant, Gary Cooper, and W.C. Fields in supporting roles?
7) *The Wizard of Oz* is based on what writer's work?
8) "Well, here's another nice mess you've gotten me into!" is from what movie?
9) Who plays *The Invisible Man*?
10) What film stars Marlene Dietrich as a woman who rediscovers a former lover during a dangerous train ride to Shanghai?

Quiz 8 Answers

1) Bashful
2) Scavenger hunt
3) Alan Hale – father of Alan Hale Jr. who played the Skipper on *Gilligan's Island*
4) Howard Hawks
5) *City Lights*
6) *Alice in Wonderland* – Grant plays the Mock Turtle; Cooper plays the White Knight, and Fields plays Humpty-Dumpty.
7) L. Frank Baum
8) *Sons of the Desert* – Oliver Hardy

9) Claude Rains
10) *Shanghai Express*

Quiz 9

1) Shirley Temple plays the title role in *Heidi*; who plays her grandfather?
2) Who plays the title role in *Cleopatra*?
3) The line "I want to be alone," is from what movie?
4) What Marx Brothers film involves a missing painting?
5) "Pay no attention to that man behind the curtain," is from what movie?
6) What character does John Wayne play in *Stagecoach*?
7) What is Gunga Din's job with the British Army?
8) What movie ends with the line "After all, tomorrow is another day"?
9) What movie has Count Zaroff hunting humans for sport on a remote island?
10) What was the first film to lose (nominated but didn't win) at least 10 Academy awards?

Quiz 9 Answers

1) Jean Hersholt
2) Claudette Colbert
3) *Grand Hotel* – Greta Garbo
4) *Animal Crackers*
5) *The Wizard of Oz* – Frank Morgan
6) Ringo Kid
7) Water bearer
8) *Gone with the Wind*
9) *The Most Dangerous Game*
10) *Mr. Smith Goes to Washington* – It was nominated for 11 Oscars and only won one; its competition that year included *Gone with the Wind*, *The Wizard of Oz*, *Wuthering Heights*, and *Stagecoach*.

Quiz 10

1) Who directed *Gone with the Wind*?
2) In Disney's *Snow White and the Seven Dwarfs*, how old is Snow White?
3) Who won a Best Actor Oscar for the title role in *The Private Life of Henry VIII*?

4) What movie features Charlie Chaplin struggling in an industrialized world?
5) What is Jimmy Stewart's full character name in *Mr. Smith Goes to Washington*?
6) Who plays the title role in *Gunga Din*?
7) Who plays the newspaper reporter in *Mr. Deeds Goes to Town*?
8) What is the real name of Edward G. Robinson's character in *Little Caesar*?
9) What was the most expensive Hollywood film made during the 1930s?
10) What is baby in *Bringing Up Baby*?

Quiz 10 Answers

1) Victor Fleming
2) 14
3) Charles Laughton
4) *Modern Times*
5) Jefferson Smith
6) Sam Jaffe
7) Jean Arthur
8) Rico
9) *Gone with the Wind* – $4 million at the time
10) Leopard

Quiz 11

1) What future television superhero plays one of Scarlett's beaus, Brent Tarleton, in *Gone with the Wind*?
2) What character did Basil Rathbone play in *The Adventures of Robin Hood*?
3) Who plays the saloon singer Frenchie in *Destry Rides Again*?
4) Who plays Long John Silver in *Treasure Island*?
5) What film is about young German soldiers facing disillusionment during WWI?
6) What comedy features a famous Walls of Jericho scene?
7) In *Saratoga*, Clark Gable plays bookie Duke Bradley who wins a stud farm and takes a shine to the daughter of the former owner; who plays the daughter in her last film role?
8) What is the profession of Cary Grant's character in *Bringing up Baby*?
9) Who plays the role of Sydney Carton in *A Tale of Two Cities*?
10) *The Wizard of Oz* lost the Best Picture Oscar to what movie?

Quiz 11 Answers

1) George Reeves – television's original Superman
2) Sir Guy of Gisbourne
3) Marlene Dietrich
4) Wallace Beery
5) *All Quiet on the Western Front*
6) *It Happened One Night* – Clark Gable and Claudette Colbert's characters build a wall with a blanket hanging on a line between their beds when they share a room.
7) Jean Harlow – She died during filming.
8) Paleontologist
9) Ronald Colman
10) *Gone with the Wind*

1940s

Quiz 1

1) After seeing John Wayne's performance in what film did director John Ford say, "I never knew the big son of a bitch could act"?
2) What Disney film features Uncle Remus telling tales of Brer Rabbit?
3) What is the title character's job in *Sullivan's Travels*?
4) What is the full name of Humphrey Bogart's character in *Casablanca*?
5) Who plays the French and American married military couple trying to get back to the U.S. in the comedy *I Was a Male War Bride*?
6) Who plays the stuffy law professor and stars with Cary Grant and Jean Arthur in *The Talk of the Town*?
7) What was Spencer Tracy and Katharine Hepburn's first film together?
8) What film pairs Spencer Tracy and Katharine Hepburn in a Presidential campaign?
9) What movie beat *Citizen Kane* for the Best Picture Oscar?
10) What film has con artists trying to take advantage of a simple millionaire played by Henry Fonda?

Quiz 1 Answers

1) Red River – The movie was directed by Howard Hawks; this led Ford to cast Wayne in future westerns.
2) *Song of the South*
3) Movie director
4) Rick Blaine
5) **Cary Grant and Ann Sheridan**
6) Ronald Colman
7) *Woman of the Year*
8) *State of the Union* – based on a Pulitzer Prize winning drama
9) *How Green Was My Valley*
10) *The Lady Eve*

Quiz 2

1) Who plays John Doe's traveling companion in *Meet John Doe*?
2) Who plays the insurance investigator in *Double Indemnity*?

3) Missing for seven years and presumed dead, a woman returns home on the day of her husband's second marriage; what is the comedy?

4) What two child actors co-starred in the first Lassie movie?

5) What film was advertised as "Greed, gold and gunplay on a Mexican mountain of malice"?

6) *The Grapes of Wrath* is based on what author's work?

7) Timothy Q. Mouse, Mr. Stork and Jim Crow are characters in what Disney film?

8) What is the name of Cary Grant's character in *Arsenic and Old Lace*?

9) What movie has the famous line "Here's looking at you kid"?

10) Who plays Susan Walker, the little girl who doesn't believe in Santa Claus, in *Miracle on 34th Street*?

Quiz 2 Answers

1) Walter Brennan
2) Edward G. Robinson
3) *My Favorite Wife*
4) Roddy McDowall and Elizabeth Taylor
5) *The Treasure of the Sierra Madre*
6) John Steinbeck
7) *Dumbo*
8) Mortimer Brewster
9) *Casablanca* – Humphrey Bogart
10) Natalie Wood

Quiz 3

1) Who plays Jack Benny's wife in *To Be or Not to Be*?

2) Who plays Babe Ruth in *The Pride of the Yankees*?

3) In *National Velvet*, how does Velvet acquire her horse?

4) Who plays the grizzled prospector in *The Treasure of the Sierra Madre*?

5) What song does Rick ask Sam to play in *Casablanca*?

6) What film features Gene Kelly and Frank Sinatra as sailors on shore leave in New York City?

7) Ma and Pa Kettle first appeared in supporting roles in *The Egg and I* in 1947 and went on to star in nine movies of their own starting with *Ma and Pa Kettle* in 1949; who played Ma and Pa Kettle?

8) What spy movie pairs Cary Grant and Ingrid Bergman?

9) Who plays Sister Mary Benedict in *The Bells of St. Mary's*?

10) "Badges? We ain't got no badges! We don't need no badges! I don't have to show you any stinking badges!" is from what film?

Quiz 3 Answers

1) Carole Lombard
2) Babe Ruth
3) She wins him in a raffle.
4) Walter Huston – His son John Huston directed the movie.
5) "As Time Goes By"
6) *On the Town*
7) Marjorie Main and Percy Kilbride
8) *Notorious*
9) Ingrid Bergman
10) *The Treasure of the Sierra Madre*

Quiz 4

1) What character sang "When You Wish Upon a Star" in Disney's *Pinocchio*?
2) Based on a novel by Somerset Maugham, what movie stars Tyrone Power as an adventurous young man who sets out to find himself?
3) In *Duel in the Sun*, Jennifer Jones is torn between two sons, one good and the other bad; who plays the bad younger son?
4) In *Remember the Night*, Barbara Stanwyck plays a shoplifter who is taken home to the prosecutor's family for Christmas and falls in love; who plays the prosecutor?
5) What character says, "Tell 'em to go out there with all they got and win just one for the Gipper"?
6) Who plays the title role in *The Secret Life of Walter Mitty*?
7) What film was based on a prize-winning radio suspense drama starring Agnes Moorehead?
8) What 1941 portrayal won Gary Cooper a Best Actor Oscar?
9) For what film did Joan Crawford win her only Oscar?
10) What movie was directed by Howard Hawks and features Humphrey Bogart and Lauren Bacall in a Raymond Chandler story?

Quiz 4 Answers

1) Jiminy Cricket
2) *The Razor's Edge*

3) Gregory Peck
4) Fred MacMurray
5) Knute Rockne – Pat O'Brien in *Knute Rockne All American*
6) Danny Kaye
7) *Sorry, Wrong Number*
8) Sergeant Alvin York
9) *Mildred Pierce* – 1945
10) *The Big Sleep*

Quiz 5

1) In what film does Orson Welles play a Nazi war criminal hiding out in Connecticut?
2) Lon Chaney Jr. plays the title role in *The Wolf Man*; what is his character's name?
3) What comedic romp features Cary Grant and Rosalind Russell and is one of the fastest talking movies ever?
4) *Bambi* was the first Disney film without what?
5) What Abbott and Costello film features two ghosts who were mistakenly branded as traitors during the Revolutionary War and return to 20th century New England to retrieve a letter from George Washington which would prove their innocence?
6) In *Arsenic and Old Lace*, Peter Lorre plays a surgeon who has altered the villain's face to look like who?
7) In which Spencer Tracy and Katharine Hepburn movie do they play married lawyers?
8) What film is set in a run-down hotel as a hurricane approaches?
9) What was the most expensive Hollywood film made during the 1940s?
10) Tyrone Power plays the title character in *The Mark of Zorro*; what is Zorro's real name?

Quiz 5 Answers

1) *The Stranger*
2) Larry Talbot
3) *His Girl Friday*
4) Human characters
5) *The Time of Their Lives*
6) Boris Karloff
7) *Adam's Rib*

8) *Key Largo*
9) *Duel in the Sun* – $8 million at the time
10) Don Diego de la Vega

Quiz 6

1) What was the first film to feature Humphrey Bogart and Lauren Bacall?
2) In the comedy *I Married a Witch*, who plays the witch opposite Fredric March?
3) What film has Charlie Chaplin playing dual roles including a Jewish barber?
4) Bing Crosby plays the title role in *A Connecticut Yankee in King Arthur's Court*; whose novel is the movie based on?
5) What movie has Lana Turner convincing a drifter to help her murder her husband?
6) What Olivia de Havilland film chronicles a woman's stay in a mental institution?
7) What is the name of Bing Crosby's character in *Going My Way*?
8) What film starring Rita Hayworth was a sequel to *Here Comes Mr. Jordan*?
9) Abbott and Costello's first starring roles are in what movie that also features the Andrews Sisters singing "Boogie Woogie Bugle Boy"?
10) What movie was based on a long-running radio show and features the first screen performance of Dean Martin and Jerry Lewis?

Quiz 6 Answers

1) *To Have and Have Not*
2) Veronica Lake
3) *The Great Dictator* – He also plays the dictator.
4) Mark Twain
5) *The Postman Always Rings Twice*
6) *The Snake Pit*
7) Father Chuck O'Malley
8) *Down to Earth*
9) *Buck Privates*
10) *My Friend Irma*

Quiz 7

1) Gary Cooper plays John Doe in *Meet John Doe*; what is the real name of his character?
2) For what film did Ray Milland win a Best Actor Oscar?
3) Who plays the young deaf-mute woman in *Johnny Belinda*?
4) What is the name of the angel played by Cary Grant in *The Bishop's Wife*?
5) What movie features John Wayne as Captain Nathan Brittles on the eve of retirement?
6) In *Ball of Fire*, Gary Cooper plays a professor who is writing what?
7) Who plays the mobster Johnny Rocco in *Key Largo*?
8) In *Sorry, Wrong Number*, who plays the husband who arranges the murder of his invalid wife played by Barbara Stanwyck?
9) Who plays General Savage who takes over a bomber unit during WWII and whips them into shape in *Twelve O'Clock High*?
10) What movie based on an Agatha Christie novel has seven guests on an isolated island being killed off one by one?

Quiz 7 Answers

1) John Willoughby
2) *The Lost Weekend*
3) Jane Wyman
4) Dudley
5) *She Wore a Yellow Ribbon*
6) An encyclopedia article on slang
7) Edward G. Robinson
8) Burt Lancaster
9) Gregory Peck
10) *And Then There Were None*

Quiz 8

1) What film is about the social adjustments faced by three returning WWII servicemen?
2) What 1942 Humphrey Bogart film won the Best Picture Oscar?
3) What movie has the protagonist planning to jump off the city hall roof at midnight on Christmas Eve?
4) What Orson Welles film was based on a Pulitzer Prize winning novel by Booth Tarkington?

5) In *Pride and Prejudice*, Greer Garson plays Elizabeth Bennet; who plays Mr. Darcy?
6) What film centers on the exploits of a conscientious objector during WWI?
7) What is the name of the angel in *It's a Wonderful Life*?
8) Who directed *It's a Wonderful Life*?
9) What was Charles Foster Kane's dying word?
10) Who plays the title roles in *The Bachelor and the Bobby-Soxer*?

Quiz 8 Answers

1) *The Best Years of Our Lives*
2) *Casablanca*
3) *Meet John Doe*
4) *The Magnificent Ambersons*
5) Laurence Olivier
6) *Sergeant York*
7) Clarence – played by Henry Travers
8) Frank Capra
9) Rosebud
10) Cary Grant and Shirley Temple

Quiz 9

1) What movie stars Henry Fonda as Wyatt Earp?
2) Loretta Young plays Katie Holstrom who leaves the farm to become a nurse but is sidetracked into domestic service, romance, and politics in what film?
3) Sydney Greenstreet and Peter Lorre made nine films together; what was the first?
4) What is the name of the skunk in Disney's *Bambi*?
5) What actress says, "Oh, Jerry, don't let's ask for the moon. We have the stars"?
6) What movie has a reporter pretending to be Jewish to write a story on anti-Semitism?
7) What movie is based on a story by Carlo Collodi?
8) Who plays the title role in *The Lady Eve*?
9) What movie stars Henry Fonda and features a mistaken lynching?
10) What Katharine Hepburn and Cary Grant film was remade as *High Society* in 1956?

Quiz 9 Answers

1) *My Darling Clementine*
2) *The Farmer's Daughter*
3) *The Maltese Falcon*
4) Flower
5) Bette Davis – *Now, Voyager*
6) *Gentleman's Agreement* – starring Gregory Peck
7) *Pinocchio*
8) Barbara Stanwyck
9) *The Ox-Bow Incident*
10) *The Philadelphia Story*

Quiz 10

1) Who plays the title role in *Gilda*?
2) What 1941 film was remade by Warren Beatty as *Heaven Can Wait* in 1978?
3) In *The Major and the Minor*, a woman disguises herself as a child to save on train fare and is taken in by an army man who doesn't realize it; who plays the woman posing as a child?
4) What sports-based movie stars Gary Cooper?
5) Who plays the wife who has trouble adapting to rural life on a chicken farm in *The Egg and I*?
6) What Alfred Hitchcock film won Joan Fontaine a Best Actress Oscar and co-stars Cary Grant as her husband she suspects is planning to kill her?
7) What instrument was used to play the unusual theme music for *The Third Man*?
8) Who plays the two doctors who fall in love in Hitchcock's *Spellbound*?
9) What is the theme song for *The Grapes of Wrath*?
10) In what film did Alec Guinness play eight parts?

Quiz 10 Answers

1) Rita Hayworth
2) *Here Comes Mr. Jordan*
3) Ginger Rogers
4) *The Pride of the Yankees*
5) Claudette Colbert
6) *Suspicion*

7) Zither – a stringed instrument
8) Gregory Peck and Ingrid Bergman
9) "The Red River Valley"
10) *Kind Hearts and Coronets*

Quiz 11

1) City apartment dwellers Cary Grant and Myrna Loy decide to build a home in the country in what comedy?
2) Anne Revere won a Best Supporting Actress Oscar for her role in what film that features a famous international sporting event?
3) What are the names of the two rival department stores in *Miracle on 34th Street*?
4) What comedy is about two men and a woman sharing a single apartment during the WWII housing shortage in Washington, D.C.?
5) What is the name of the character that keeps Pinocchio in a cage?
6) What was the first of the seven Bing Crosby and Bob Hope *Road* pictures?
7) What George Cukor psychological thriller stars Ingrid Bergman, Charles Boyer, and Joseph Cotten?
8) What movie features the line "The stuff that dreams are made of"?
9) "Made it, Ma! Top of the world!" is from what film?
10) What film has a notorious gunman played by John Wayne being nursed back to health by a Quaker family?

Quiz 11 Answers

1) *Mr. Blandings Builds His Dream House*
2) *National Velvet* – She plays Velvet's mother.
3) Macy's and Gimbels
4) *The More the Merrier*
5) Stromboli
6) *Road to Singapore*
7) *Gaslight*
8) *The Maltese Falcon* – Humphrey Bogart
9) *White Heat* – James Cagney
10) *The Angel and the Badman*

Quiz 12

1) *All the King's Men* is based on the life of what politician?

2) What Hitchcock film features Joan Fontaine and Laurence Olivier?

3) Edmund O'Brien plays Frank Bigelow who has been poisoned and only has a few days to live and tries to find out who killed him and why in what film?

4) Who plays the title role in *The Bishop's Wife*?

5) In *National Velvet*, what is the name of Velvet Brown's horse?

6) What movie stars James Cagney as psychopathic criminal Cody Jarrett?

7) Who plays the adult adopted son of John Wayne's character in *Red River*?

8) What is the name of Jimmy Stewart's character in *It's a Wonderful Life*?

9) What newspaper owner's career inspired *Citizen Kane*?

10) What was the number one U.S. box office film released in the 1940s?

Quiz 12 Answers

1) Huey Long – Louisiana governor

2) *Rebecca*

3) *D.O.A.*

4) Loretta Young – David Niven plays the bishop.

5) The Pie

6) *White Heat*

7) Montgomery Clift

8) George Bailey

9) William Randolph Hearst

10) *Bambi* – 1942

Quiz 13

1) In *National Velvet*, Velvet's mother provides the entrance fee for the horse race out of her prize money for doing what?

2) Who plays the female judge who eventually falls for Cary Grant's character in *The Bachelor and the Bobby-Soxer*?

3) What Hitchcock film deals heavily with psychoanalysis?

4) Who does James Cagney portray in *Yankee Doodle Dandy*?

5) In *Easter Parade*, Fred Astaire plays a dancer who loses a partner; who plays his new partner?

6) What actor plays the matchmaker to Jean Arthur and Joel McCrea's characters in *The More the Merrier*?

7) What film stars Don Ameche arriving at the gates of Hell to be judged?

8) What character does Humphrey Bogart play in *The Maltese Falcon*?

9) Who plays the title role in *Jane Eyre* opposite Orson Welles as Edward Rochester?

10) Bette Davis stars in the story of the ruthless, rich Hubbard clan in the deep South at the turn of the 20th century in what movie?

Quiz 13 Answers

1) Swimming the English Channel
2) Myrna Loy
3) *Spellbound*
4) George M. Cohan
5) Judy Garland
6) Charles Coburn
7) *Heaven Can Wait*
8) Sam Spade
9) Joan Fontaine
10) *The Little Foxes*

Quiz 14

1) In what film did Orson Welles play the character Harry Lime?

2) Robert Young plays a disfigured Air Force pilot and Dorothy McGuire is a shy, homely maid who gradually fall in love and discover that their feelings for each other have mysteriously transformed them in what film?

3) How old was Orson Welles when he co-wrote, produced, directed and starred in *Citizen Kane*?

4) Who directed *The Philadelphia Story*?

5) What comedy is set in occupied Poland during WWII and features a group of stage actors matching wits with the Nazis?

6) What is the name of the family in *The Grapes of Wrath*?

7) Who plays Kris Kringle in *Miracle on 34th Street*?

8) What is Cary Grant's character name in *The Talk of the Town*?

9) Who plays Mrs. Muir in *The Ghost and Mrs. Muir*?

10) Who was the classical music conductor for the music in *Fantasia*?

Quiz 14 Answers

1) *The Third Man*
2) *The Enchanted Cottage*
3) 25

4) George Cukor
5) *To Be or Not to Be*
6) Joad
7) Edmund Gwenn
8) Leopold Dilg
9) Gene Tierney
10) Leopold Stokowski

Quiz 15

1) In Hitchcock's *Shadow of a Doubt*, who plays Charlie Oakley, the Merry Widow Murderer?
2) Ray Milland plays a scientist who discovers s substance that causes a baseball to be repelled by wood and takes a leave of absence to become a major league pitcher in what comedy?
3) What is the name of the town that is the setting for *It's a Wonderful Life*?
4) In *The Man Who Came to Dinner*, acerbic critic Sheridan Whiteside slips on the front steps of a prominent Ohio family's home and insists on recuperating in their home during Christmas; Bette Davis plays the critic's assistant; who plays the title role?
5) An inventor needs cash to develop his big idea, so his wife decides to raise it by divorcing him and marrying a millionaire; what is this Preston Sturges comedy?
6) Who plays the woman accused of attempted murder in *Adam's Rib*?
7) In *The Ghost and Mrs. Muir*, what is the name of the cottage where Mrs. Muir lives?
8) What film has W.C. Fields playing a henpecked husband who with no experience gets hired as a substitute film director?
9) In the Biblical tale *Samson and Delilah*, who plays the strongman Samson?
10) What movie features David Niven as a British WWII aviator who cheats death through a heavenly mistake and must argue for his life before a celestial court?

Quiz 15 Answers

1) Joseph Cotton
2) *It Happens Every Spring*
3) Bedford Falls
4) Monty Woolley
5) *The Palm Beach Story*

6) Judy Holiday
7) Gull Cottage
8) *The Bank Dick*
9) Victor Mature
10) *A Matter of Life and Death*

Quiz 16

1) Who wrote the Pulitzer Prize winning novel *All the King's Men* upon which the movie was based?
2) What movie is set during the Spanish Civil War and based on an Ernest Hemingway novel?
3) What prominent long-time stage actor had his film debut in *The Maltese Falcon*?
4) What movie focuses on four daughters in the year leading up to a World's Fair?
5) Who plays the Civil War veteran father in *The Yearling*?
6) What character says, "**Today, I consider myself the luckiest man on the face of the earth**"?
7) What Cary Grant and Katharine Hepburn movie is about a young man planning to take a break from work to find himself who falls in love with his fiancée's sister?
8) What were the three 1940s musicals featuring Frank Sinatra and Gene Kelly?
9) What Hitchcock movie is about two college students who try to perform the perfect murder?
10) What was the sequel to *Going My Way*?

Quiz 16 Answers

1) Robert Penn Warren
2) *For Whom the Bell Tolls*
3) Sydney Greenstreet
4) *Meet Me in St. Louis*
5) Gregory Peck
6) Lou Gehrig – played by Gary Cooper in *The Pride of the Yankees*
7) *Holiday*
8) *Anchors Aweigh*, *Take Me Out to the Ball Game*, *On the Town*
9) *Rope*
10) *The Bells of St. Mary's*

1950s

Quiz 1

1) Who plays artist Henri de Toulouse-Lautrec in *Moulin Rouge*?
2) Who plays the title characters in *Solomon and Sheba*?
3) What Alfred Hitchcock comedy revolves around a dead body found in the woods?
4) In what century is *The Ten Commandments* set?
5) Who won a Best Supporting Actress Oscar for her film debut in *On the Waterfront*?
6) Who plays the junkyard tycoon Harry Brock in *Born Yesterday*?
7) In what western does the character Will Kane appear?
8) What was Elvis Presley's first feature film?
9) What Best Picture Oscar winner has no spoken words in the last 20 minutes and 25 seconds of the film?
10) What Hitchcock film has two strangers trading murders?

Quiz 1 Answers

1) Jose Ferrer
2) Yul Brynner and Gina Lollobrigida
3) *The Trouble with Harry*
4) 13th century BC
5) Eva Marie Saint
6) Broderick Crawford
7) *High Noon*
8) *Love Me Tender*
9) *An American in Paris*
10) *Strangers on a Train*

Quiz 2

1) Who wrote the play upon which *Cat on a Hot Tin Roof* is based?
2) In *House of Wax*, Vincent Price plays a disfigured sculptor who rebuilds his wax museum by murdering people and using their wax covered corpses as displays; who plays his deaf-mute helper Igor?
3) Judy Holliday and Jack Lemmon star in the story of a young woman who dreams of fame and rents a billboard to advertise herself and

changes her life overnight; what is the film?

4) What film has the line "Fasten your seatbelts. It's going to be a bumpy night"?

5) What Best Picture Oscar winner is about an ingenue who insinuates herself into the life of an aging Broadway star?

6) What is the romantic comedy starring Katharine Hepburn and Spencer Tracy that is set in what is now the NBC headquarters at 30 Rockefeller Center?

7) In *The Nun's Story*, a woman leaves her wealthy Belgian family to become a nun and is assigned to work in the Congo; who plays the title character Sister Luke?

8) King Solomon's Mines marked the first time what African tribe allowed themselves to be filmed?

9) Who plays the role of Big Daddy in *Cat on a Hot Tin Roof*?

10) Who won a Best Supporting Actress Oscar for *The Diary of Anne Frank*?

Quiz 2 Answers

1) Tennessee Williams
2) Charles Bronson
3) *It Should Happen to You*
4) *All About Eve* – Bette Davis
5) *All About Eve*
6) *Desk Set*
7) Audrey Hepburn
8) Watusi
9) Burl Ives
10) Shelley Winters

Quiz 3

1) Who plays Gary Cooper's much younger wife in *High Noon*?

2) Walt Disney's *Peter Pan* is based on a play by what novelist and playwright?

3) In what Hitchcock film does Doris Day sing the Oscar winning song "Que Sera, Sera"?

4) What actors were chained together in *The Defiant Ones*?

5) In *Love is a Many Splendored Thing*, who plays the starring roles of an American reporter and a widowed Chinese physician who fall in love?

6) What is the name of the river Humphrey Bogart and Katharine Hepburn navigate in *The African Queen*?

7) Spencer Tracy plays the father in *Father of the Bride*; who plays the bride?

8) Who stars as Lonesome Rhodes, a drifter who becomes an overnight media sensation, in *A Face in the Crowd*?

9) What western stars John Wayne as Ethan Edwards looking for his abducted niece?

10) Who plays Anna in 1956's *The King and I*?

Quiz 3 Answers

1) Grace Kelly
2) J.M. Barrie
3) *The Man Who Knew Too Much*
4) Tony Curtis and Sidney Poitier
5) William Holden and Jennifer Jones
6) Ulanga River
7) Elizabeth Taylor
8) Andy Griffith
9) *The Searchers* – directed by John Ford
10) Deborah Kerr

Quiz 4

1) What Oscar winning film centers on a runaway princess who falls in love with a newsman?

2) What were James Dean's three films?

3) For what film did Burl Ives win a Best Supporting Actor Oscar?

4) Who plays the German informer in *Stalag 17*?

5) What film based on a Tennessee Williams play stars Katharine Hepburn, Elizabeth Taylor, and Montgomery Clift?

6) What science fiction film was loosely based on Shakespeare's *The Tempest* and was the film debut of Leslie Nielsen?

7) What 1954 film won eight Oscars?

8) What was the number one U.S. box office film released in the 1950s?

9) Who are the three singing and dancing stars of *Singin' in the Rain*?

10) Based on a novel by James Michener, what Marlon Brando film has the tagline "Worlds apart...theirs was the daring love affair violating every rule, every custom, every centuries-old belief!"?

Quiz 4 Answers

1) *Roman Holiday* – starring Gregory Peck and Audrey Hepburn
2) *Rebel Without a Cause, East of Eden, Giant*
3) *The Big Country*
4) Peter Graves
5) *Suddenly, Last Summer*
6) *Forbidden Planet*
7) *On the Waterfront*
8) *The Ten Commandments* – 1956
9) Gene Kelly, Donald O'Connor, Debbie Reynolds – Reynolds was only 19 at the time; she had no prior dance experience and commuted to the set by bus from her parent's home where she lived.
10) *Sayonara*

Quiz 5

1) What is the name of the witch in Disney's *Sleeping Beauty*?
2) What is the former profession of Jahn Wayne's character in *The Quiet Man*?
3) Who are the two actors in the famous beach scene in *From Here to Eternity*?
4) What movie has the tiny country of Grand Fenwick declaring war on the U.S.?
5) For what film did Judy Holliday win her only Best Actress Oscar?
6) What film has John Wayne, Dean Martin, Ricky Nelson, and Walter Brennan trying to keep an accused murderer in jail?
7) Who co-stars with Cary Grant in *Houseboat*?
8) Who plays the title role in *Ivanhoe*?
9) Who has the title role in *Sabrina*?
10) Victor Mature plays a Christian slave sent to fight in the gladiatorial arena, and Emperor Caligula seeks Jesus' robe in what film?

Quiz 5 Answers

1) Maleficent
2) Boxer
3) Burt Lancaster and Deborah Kerr
4) *The Mouse That Roared*
5) *Born Yesterday*

6) *Rio Bravo*
7) Sophia Loren
8) Robert Taylor
9) Audrey Hepburn
10) *Demetrius and the Gladiators*

Quiz 6

1) Who plays the man James Stewart's character believes has murdered his wife in *Rear Window*?
2) What actor provides the voice for Francis the talking mule?
3) Who plays Princess Aouda, Phileas Fogg's love interest, in *Around the World in 80 Days*?
4) What film based on an Ernest Hemingway novel stars Gregory Peck as writer Harry Street?
5) What two actors play the two brothers who both fall in love with the title character in *Sabrina*?
6) What Cary Grant and Tony Curtis comedy revolves around a WWII submarine?
7) Gregory Peck stars as Jimmy Ringo, a notorious gunman, in what movie?
8) In his only credited directing role, what well known actor directed *The Night of the Hunter*?
9) Who plays the leader of the criminal gang planning a bank robbery in the comedy *The Ladykillers*?
10) *On the Beach* starring Gregory Peck is about the aftermath of a nuclear WWIII; what country is in set in?

Quiz 6 Answers

1) Raymond Burr
2) Chill Wills
3) Shirley MacLaine
4) *The Snows of Kilimanjaro*
5) Humphrey Bogart and William Holden
6) *Operation Petticoat*
7) *The Gunfighter*
8) Charles Laughton
9) Alec Guinness
10) Australia

Quiz 7

1) What western character actor who appeared in films such as *High Noon* had a Billboard number one hit song in 1958?
2) What is the name of James Stewart's character in *Harvey*?
3) What William Wyler western stars Gregory Peck, Charlton Heston, Jean Simmons, Burl Ives, and Chuck Connors?
4) Who stars as Dr. Miles Bennell in the *Invasion of the Body Snatchers*?
5) Who plays Charlton Heston's mother in both *The Ten Commandments* and *Ben-Hur*?
6) In *To Catch a Thief*, Cary Grant's character is a retired thief; what is his criminal nickname?
7) Robert Taylor and Deborah Kerr star in what film about a Roman commander who becomes infatuated with a beautiful Christian hostage and begins questioning the tyrannical leadership of the Emperor Nero?
8) What romantic comedy stars Judy Holliday and Jack Lemmon as a married couple who decide to go their separate ways?
9) The actor who plays the boy befriended by the alien in *The Day the Earth Stood Still* later starred as the son in a famous television family; who is he?
10) What movie features seven warriors protecting a village?

Quiz 7 Answers

1) Sheb Wooley – "The Purple People Eater"
2) Elwood P. Dowd
3) *The Big Country*
4) Kevin McCarthy
5) Martha Scott
6) The Cat
7) *Quo Vadis*
8) *Phffft*
9) Billy Gray – He also appeared as Bud Anderson in *Father Knows Best*.
10) *Seven Samurai*

Quiz 8

1) In Hitchcock's *North by Northwest*, who plays Cary Grant's love interest?
2) What mythical Scottish town appears for one day every hundred years?
3) For what film did Gary Cooper win his second Best Actor Oscar?
4) Whose life was depicted in *To Hell and Back*?

5) What is the name of the character played by John Wayne in *The Quiet Man*?

6) In *Ben-Hur*, what is the title character's first name?

7) What was James Dean's last movie?

8) In what country is Alfred Hitchcock's *The Man Who Knew Too Much* set?

9) What science fiction film has giant mutant ants?

10) *Dumbo* was Disney's first movie based on an original story; what was the second Disney film based on an original story?

Quiz 8 Answers

1) Eve Marie Saint
2) *Brigadoon*
3) *High Noon*
4) Audie Murphy – most decorated American soldier in WWII
5) Sean Thornton
6) Judah
7) *Giant* – He died before it was released.
8) Morocco
9) *Them!*
10) *Lady and the Tramp*

Quiz 9

1) Who wrote the novel upon which the film *Ivanhoe* is based?

2) In *The Day the Earth Stood Still*, what is the name of the alien?

3) What was the most expensive Hollywood film made during the 1950s?

4) Who plays the role of a preacher and murderer in *The Night of the Hunter*?

5) What film is a musical remake of *The Philadelphia Story*?

6) Who is Ben Hur's rival in the great chariot race?

7) What is the occupation of the title character in *Marty*?

8) Spencer Tracy plays a one-armed stranger arriving in a tiny Arizona town with a dark secret in what movie?

9) For what 1955 film did Jack Lemmon win his first Oscar?

10) Who plays Phileas Fogg's manservant Passepartout in *Around the World in 80 Days*?

Quiz 9 Answers

1) Sir Walter Scott

2) Klaatu
3) *Ben-Hur* – $15 million at the time
4) Robert Mitchum
5) *High Society*
6) Messala
7) Butcher
8) *Bad Day at Black Rock*
9) *Mister Roberts*
10) Cantinflas

Quiz 10

1) In the romantic comedy *Teacher's Pet*, Clark Gable plays the student; who plays the teacher?
2) Who plays the oldest brother Adam in *Seven Brides for Seven Brothers*?
3) In Disney's Cinderella, who provides Prince Charming's singing voice?
4) For what movie did Sidney Poitier receive his first Best Actor Oscar nomination?
5) In *War of the Worlds*, where does the initial Martin spacecraft come down?
6) What kind of whale is Moby Dick?
7) What is the name of Captain Ahab's ship in *Moby Dick*?
8) What is the name of the adventurer Stewart Granger plays in *King Solomon's Mines*?
9) In *How to Marry a Millionaire*, what three actresses play the lead roles of the young women looking for love?
10) In *The Caine Mutiny*, what does Humphrey Bogart's character roll in his hand when he becomes frustrated or unsure of himself?

Quiz 10 Answers

1) Doris Day
2) Howard Keel
3) Mike Douglas – best known for his television talk show *The Mike Douglas Show*
4) *The Defiant Ones*
5) California – east of Los Angeles
6) Sperm whale
7) Pequod
8) Allan Quartermain

9) Marilyn Monroe, Betty Grable, Lauren Bacall
10) Steel balls

Quiz 11

1) Alan Ladd frequently played heroes; his height required some adjustments in some of his films to make him appear larger than he was; how tall was he?
2) Frank Sinatra stars as a card dealer and former heroin addict who returns home after six months of incarceration and rehab and tries to find a new livelihood and avoid slipping back into addiction in what movie?
3) *A Night to Remember* is about what famous event?
4) What is the title song which won an Oscar for *High Noon*?
5) Who plays the gunslinger Jack Wilson brought in to kill the title character in *Shane*?
6) What is the name of Humphrey Bogart's character in *The Caine Mutiny*?
7) Who plays Ishmael in *Moby Dick*?
8) Who directed *The Bridge on the River Kwai*?
9) What Disney film has Tommy Kirk and a dog in 1860s Texas?
10) In *20,000 Leagues Under the Sea*, who plays Captain Nemo?

Quiz 11 Answers

1) 5 feet 6 inches
2) *The Man with the Golden Arm*
3) Sinking of the *Titanic*
4) "Do Not Forsake Me" or "The Ballad of High Noon" – sung by Tex Ritter
5) Jack Palance
6) Captain Queeg
7) Richard Basehart
8) David Lean
9) *Old Yeller*
10) James Mason

Quiz 12

1) In *White Christmas*, what two actresses play the sister act who become romantically involved with Bing Crosby and Danny Kaye?
2) Who plays the role of Pharaoh Rameses II in *The Ten Commandments*?

3) Who is the female singer who provides her voice to *Disney's Lady and the Tramp*?
4) What is the name of the robot in *The Day the Earth Stood Still*?
5) What is the name of Marlon Brando's character in *A Streetcar Named Desire*?
6) What is the name of Humphrey Bogart's character in *The African Queen*?
7) Who plays the title role in *Gigi*?
8) In *Mister Roberts*, what do Lieutenant Roberts and Ensign Pulver both throw overboard at different times to enrage Captain Morton?
9) What was Jean Arthur's last film?
10) Who plays the wheeler-dealer J.J. Sefton in *Stalag 17*?

Quiz 12 Answers

1) Rosemary Clooney and Vera-Ellen
2) Yul Brynner
3) Peggy Lee
4) Gort
5) Stanley Kowalski
6) Charlie Allnut
7) Leslie Caron
8) The Captain's palm tree
9) *Shane* – 1953
10) William Holden

Quiz 13

1) James Mason and Pat Boone star in *Journey to the Center of the Earth*; whose novel is the movie based on?
2) In *Harvey*, the title character is a 6-foot-3 ½-inch invisible rabbit described as being an Irish folklore creature called a what?
3) What film centers on three American women rooming together while living abroad and hoping for love and marriage?
4) What film features the character of former silent screen star Norma Desmond?
5) In *The Bridge on the River Kwai*, the prisoners whistle to a marching song; what is the name of the song?
6) What movie is about the emotions stirred up when a drifter arrives in a small Kansas town on Labor Day?
7) What 1956 film caused riots in theaters?

8) In *Somebody Up There Likes Me*, Paul Newman plays what boxing champion?
9) What was Gregory Peck's first comedic movie?
10) "Well, nobody's perfect!" is the last line of what comedy?

Quiz 13 Answers

1) Jules Verne
2) Pooka
3) *Three Coins in the Fountain*
4) *Sunset Boulevard* – starting Gloria Swanson
5) Colonel Bogey March – It was written in 1914 by a British army bandmaster.
6) *Picnic* – starring Kim Novak and William Holden
7) *Rock Around the Clock*
8) Rocky Graziano
9) *Roman Holiday*
10) *Some Like It Hot*

Quiz 14

1) In *Mister Roberts*, what is the name of the cargo ship they serve on?
2) What actor was Joey Starrett yelling to when he said, "Shane! Shane! Come back!"?
3) In what country is John Wayne's *The Quiet Man* set?
4) Who wrote the Pulitzer Prize winning novel of the same name upon which *The Caine Mutiny* is based?
5) Who made her screen debut in Alfred Hitchcock's *The Trouble with Harry*?
6) Alec Guinness plays a chemist who invents a fabric that never gets dirty or wears out, but both business and labor want to suppress it for economic reasons; what is the movie?
7) Who plays the scientist who has a horrific accident while experimenting with teleportation in *The Fly*?
8) What country is *The King and I* set in?
9) For what film did John Ford win his last of four Best Director Oscars?
10) What film took place in 1943 Burma?

Quiz 14 Answers

1) *Reluctant*

2) Alan Ladd – *Shane*
3) Ireland
4) Herman Wouk
5) Shirley MacLaine
6) *The Man in the White Suit*
7) David Hedison
8) Siam – current day Thailand
9) *The Quiet Man* – 1952
10) *The Bridge on the River Kwai*

Quiz 15

1) What type of fish does the old man battle for three days and nights in *The Old Man and the Sea*?
2) James Stewart has the title role in *The Glenn Miller Story*; who plays his wife?
3) What 1953 Marlon Brando film was banned in British theaters for 14 years?
4) In *Witness for the Prosecution*, a veteran British barrister must defend his client in a murder trial that has surprise after surprise; who plays the barrister?
5) In *Annie Get Your Gun*, who plays the title role?
6) Who plays the dual roles of Madeleine Elster and Judy Barton in *Vertigo*?
7) Who stars as Scrooge in the 1951 version of *A Christmas Carol*?
8) *A Streetcar Named Desire* received Oscar acting nominations in all four categories and won three; who was nominated but didn't win an Oscar?
9) In what movie was Bill Haley's "Rock Around the Clock" first heard?
10) What western stars Alan Ladd, Jean Arthur, and Van Heflin?

Quiz 15 Answers

1) Marlin
2) June Allyson
3) *The Wild One* – It was deemed too violent to show.
4) Charles Laughton
5) Betty Hutton
6) Kim Novak
7) Alastair Sim
8) Marlon Brando

9) *Blackboard Jungle*
10) *Shane*

Quiz 16

1) Who plays the infant Moses in *The Ten Commandments*?
2) What 1950s movie is often credited as the first modern action film using elements such as slow motion for dramatic effect?
3) What film has the line "I coulda been a contender"?
4) "All right, Mr. DeMille, I'm ready for my close-up," is from what film?
5) What Best Picture Oscar winner is set in Hawaii around the time of the Japanese attack on Pearl Harbor?
6) Based on a novel by Grace Metallous, what film is about a peaceful New England town that hides secrets and scandals?
7) In what movie does Marilyn Monroe's iconic scene with her white dress blowing upward while she stands on a subway grate take place?
8) What film starring Judy Garland was a remake of a 1937 film with Janet Gaynor and was remade again in 1976 with Barbra Streisand?
9) What is the name of the Princess in Disney's *Sleeping Beauty*?
10) In *Creature from the Black Lagoon*, who plays the woman the creature falls in love with?

Quiz 16 Answers

1) Fraser Clarke Heston – Charlton Heston's son
2) *Seven Samurai*
3) *On the Waterfront* – Marlon Brando
4) *Sunset Boulevard* – Gloria Swanson
5) *From Here to Eternity*
6) *Peyton Place*
7) *The Seven Year Itch*
8) *A Star Is Born*
9) Aurora
10) Julie Adams

Quiz 17

1) *East of Eden* starring James Dean is based on whose novel?
2) Who plays the army lieutenant accused of murder in *Anatomy of a Murder*?
3) Who plays James Dean's love interest in *Rebel Without a Cause*?

4) What film is considered John Wayne and Howard Hawks' reply to *High Noon*?

5) What two actresses play the two showgirls Lorelei Lee and Dorothy Shaw in *Gentlemen Prefer Blondes*?

6) What Hitchcock film has Henry Fonda playing an innocent man mistakenly arrested for armed robbery?

7) What three 1950s Alfred Hitchcock films did Grace Kelly appear in?

8) What film stars David Niven, Rita Hayworth, Deborah Kerr, Wendy Hiller, and Burt Lancaster and tells the stories of several people staying at a seaside hotel in Bournemouth?

9) Yul Brynner won his only Best Actor Oscar for what movie?

10) What film is about a Roman tribune ordered to crucify Jesus Christ?

Quiz 17 Answers

1) John Steinbeck

2) Ben Gazzara

3) Natalie Wood

4) *Rio Bravo* – Neither Wayne nor Hawks thought a real lawman would want or need to ask for help as Gary Cooper's character did in *High Noon*.

5) Marilyn Monroe and Jane Russell

6) *The Wrong Man*

7) *Rear Window* (1954), *Dial M for Murder* (1954), *To Catch a Thief* (1955)

8) *Separate Tables*

9) *The King and I*

10) *The Robe* – starring Richard Burton

Quiz 18

1) Who plays Wyatt Earp in *Gunfight at the O.K. Corral*?

2) "Life is a banquet, and most poor suckers are starving to death!" is from what film?

3) What musical comedy features "The Oldest Established Permanent Floating Crap Game in New York"?

4) Who won a Best Actor Oscar for *Marty*?

5) What film centers on a meek bank clerk trying to steal gold bars and smuggle them out of the country as miniature Eiffel Towers?

6) All but three minutes of what film were shot inside a 16 foot by 24 foot room?

7) What Doris Day and Rock Hudson romantic comedy features Day's only

Oscar nominated performance?

8) Who plays Buttons the Clown in *The Greatest Show on Earth*?

9) Who plays the abducted niece in John Ford's western *The Searchers*?

10) Gregory Peck stars as a former WWII officer who is still tormented by memories of the war and faces ethical questions as he tries to earn enough to support his wife and children in what movie?

Quiz 18 Answers

1) Burt Lancaster
2) *Auntie Mame* – Rosalind Russell
3) *Guys and Dolls*
4) Ernest Borgnine
5) *The Lavender Hill Mob* – starring Alec Guinness
6) *12 Angry Men*
7) *Pillow Talk*
8) James Stewart – He plays the entire movie in his clown makeup.
9) Natalie Wood
10) *The Man in the Gray Flannel Suit*

1960s

Quiz 1

1) What Sergio Leone western stars Henry Fonda, Claudia Cardinale, and Charles Bronson?
2) How many roles does Peter Sellers play in *Dr. Strangelove or: How I Learned to Stop Worrying and Love the Bomb*?
3) What film is set in and around 17 Cherry Tree Lane, London in 1910?
4) What two historical figures are portrayed by Peter O'Toole and Katharine Hepburn in *The Lion in Winter*?
5) In *To Sir, with Love*, what is the name of Sidney Poitier's character?
6) What is the name of Dustin Hoffman's character in *The Graduate*?
7) What actors play the husband and wife in *A Raisin in the Sun*?
8) Who plays the teacher put on trial for teaching evolution in *Inherit the Wind*?
9) What was Clint Eastwood's character called in *The Good, the Bad and the Ugly*?
10) Who plays the psychopathic character Maggott in *The Dirty Dozen*?

Quiz 1 Answers

1) *Once Upon a Time in the West*
2) Three – Group Captain Lionel Mandrake, President Merkin Muffley, Dr. Strangelove
3) *Mary Poppins*
4) King Henry II and Queen Eleanor of Aquitaine
5) Mark Thackeray
6) Benjamin Braddock
7) Sidney Poitier and Ruby Dee – They also played husband and wife in *Buck and the Preacher* in 1972.
8) Dick York – It was his last feature film.
9) Blondie
10) Telly Savalas

Quiz 2

1) In what Elvis film does he play a Hawaiian fisherman trying to buy a boat?
2) In *It's a Mad, Mad, Mad, Mad World*, who plays the character who dies at

the beginning of the film and provides the clue that kicks off the chase for the money?

3) Charlton Heston plays the title character of a fabled Spanish hero who defends Christian Spain against the Moors in what film?

4) What year was Clint Eastwood's first spaghetti western made?

5) What actor rode the bomb down in *Dr. Strangelove or: How I Learned to Stop Worrying and Love the Bomb*?

6) What suspense thriller has Frank Sinatra as a U.S. Army major believing that one of his men may be a brainwashed Chinese agent?

7) How does Dr. Zhivago die at the end of the movie?

8) What movie has the line "Gentlemen, you can't fight in here! This is the War Room!"?

9) Who won a Best Supporting Actor Oscar for *Spartacus*?

10) *The Magnificent Seven* is based on what 1954 film?

Quiz 2 Answers

1) *Girls! Girls! Girls!*
2) Jimmy Durante
3) *El Cid*
4) 1964 – *A Fistful of Dollars*
5) Slim Pickens
6) *The Manchurian Candidate*
7) He has a fatal heart attack chasing after Lara.
8) *Dr. Strangelove or: How I Learned to Stop Worrying and Love the Bomb* – Peter Sellers
9) Peter Ustinov
10) *Seven Samurai*

Quiz 3

1) In the western comedy *The Scalphunters*, Burt Lancaster loses his furs to Indians; he is left with a well-educated escaped slave and sets out to recover his furs. Who plays the slave?

2) In *Taming of the Shrew*, who plays the shrew?

3) What movie cast includes James Garner, Steve McQueen, Charles Bronson, Donald Pleasance, and James Coburn?

4) What was the first James Bond film?

5) What two siblings both received Oscar acting nominations for separate 1966 films?

6) In what film did Benny Hill play a toymaker?

7) Barbra Streisand plays what real life performer in *Funny Girl*?
8) Who sang the title song in *To Sir, with Love*?
9) Rita Moreno won a Best Supporting Actress Oscar for what movie?
10) What Disney film has the tagline "They turned a lost island into an exotic paradise!"?

Quiz 3 Answers

1) Ossie Davis
2) Elizabeth Taylor
3) *The Great Escape*
4) *Dr. No*
5) Vanessa Redgrave for *Morgan!* and Lynn Redgrave for *Georgy Girl*
6) *Chitty Chitty Bang Bang*
7) Fanny Brice
8) Lulu
9) *West Side Story*
10) *Swiss Family Robinson*

Quiz 4

1) What musical won the Best Picture Oscar in 1968?
2) Who plays the demolitions expert in *The Guns of Navarone*?
3) What Kirk Douglas film was about an actual historical figure from about 100 BC?
4) Anne Bancroft won a Best Actress Oscar playing what character?
5) In the James Bond movies, who is the only actress to play Bond's wife?
6) In *The Sound of Music*, what branch of the military does Captain von Trapp belong to?
7) *Fahrenheit 451* is based on a novel of the same name written by what author?
8) In *The Man Who Shot Liberty Valance*, what is the name of the character James Stewart plays?
9) In *Cool Hand Luke*, the title character played by Paul Newman bets he can eat how many hard-boiled eggs in one hour?
10) Who plays Hitler in the play within the movie *The Producers*?

Quiz 4 Answers

1) *Oliver!*
2) David Niven

3) *Spartacus*
4) Anne Sullivan – *The Miracle Worker*
5) Diana Rigg – *On Her Majesty's Secret Service*
6) Navy – Even though Austria is landlocked, there was a combined Austro-Hungarian Navy at the time.
7) Ray Bradbury
8) Ransom Stoddard
9) 50
10) Dick Shawn

Quiz 5

1) What actor has the male lead in Hitchcock's *The Birds*?
2) What was the last animated film personally supervised by Walt Disney?
3) What was the second James Bond movie?
4) Who plays Dr. Strangelove?
5) Who plays Christ in *The Greatest Story Ever Told*?
6) Who plays Paul Newman's father in *Hud* and won a Best Supporting Actor Oscar for the role?
7) What suspense thriller stars Cary Grant, Audrey Hepburn, Walter Matthau, James Coburn, and George Kennedy?
8) In *Hello Dolly*, what is the name of Walter Matthau's character?
9) What film features young boys who crash land on an island and revert to savagery?
10) What two individuals created the music and lyrics for *West Side Story*?

Quiz 5 Answers

1) Rod Taylor
2) *The Jungle Book* – 1967
3) *From Russia with Love*
4) Peter Sellers
5) Max Von Sydow
6) Melvyn Douglas
7) *Charade*
8) Horace Vandergelder
9) *Lord of the Flies*
10) Leonard Bernstein and Stephen Sondheim

Quiz 6

1) Who won the only Oscar for *Cool Hand Luke*?
2) Who stars as the American cowboy Orvil Newton in *Those Magnificent Men in Their Flying Machines or How I Flew from London to Paris in 25 Hours 11 minutes*?
3) What actor led *The Dirty Dozen*?
4) What Blake Edwards comedy has the characters The Great Leslie and Professor Fate competing against each other?
5) What classic literature is the basis for *West Side Story*?
6) What are the names of the three tunnels being dug in *The Great Escape*?
7) Who plays the role of Mrs. Robinson in *The Graduate*?
8) Elizabeth Taylor plays a middle-aged wife in an abusive relationship and won her second Best Actress Oscar for what film?
9) Who plays Audrey Hepburn's husband Doc in *Breakfast at Tiffany's*?
10) In the film *In the Heat of the Night*, Virgil Tibbs is a homicide detective in what city?

Quiz 6 Answers

1) George Kennedy – Best Supporting Actor Oscar
2) Stuart Whitman
3) Lee Marvin
4) *The Great Race* – starring Tony Curtis and Jack Lemmon
5) *Romeo and Juliet*
6) Tom, Dick, Harry
7) Anne Bancroft
8) *Who's Afraid of Virginia Woolf?*
9) Buddy Ebsen
10) Philadelphia

Quiz 7

1) What is the significance of the title *Fahrenheit 451*?
2) Who wrote the novel on which *Lord of the Flies* is based?
3) In *The Courtship of Eddie's Father*, who plays the young son Eddie who wants to see his father remarry?
4) What movie features Walter Matthau as a dentist who fakes being married to avoid commitment and recruits his nurse to pose as his wife?
5) Who plays the title character in *Zorba the Greek*?

6) *A Man for All Seasons* deals with the relationship between what two historical figures?
7) Who plays Jerry Lewis' love interest in *The Nutty Professor*?
8) What three actors play *The Good, The Bad, and The Ugly*?
9) What is the name of Zero Mostel's character in *The Producers*?
10) Who plays the Bond villain Ernst Stavro Blofeld in *On Her Majesty's Secret Service*?

Quiz 7 Answers

1) It is the temperature at which book paper catches fire and burns.
2) William Golding
3) Ron Howard
4) *Cactus Flower* – costarring Ingrid Bergman and Goldie Hawn
5) Anthony Quinn
6) Sir Thomas More and King Henry VIII
7) Stella Stevens
8) Clint Eastwood, Lee Van Cleef, Eli Wallach
9) Max Bialystock
10) Telly Savalas

Quiz 8

1) In what Alfred Hitchcock film did Julie Andrews star with Paul Newman?
2) For what role did Burt Lancaster win a Best Actor Oscar?
3) In *Goldfinger*, what is Goldfinger's first name?
4) Blind Audrey Hepburn is terrorized by thugs looking for what in *Wait Until Dark*?
5) *The Guns of Navarone* is based on a novel by what author?
6) Who plays the leader of the Russian team that goes onshore in the comedy *The Russians Are Coming! The Russians Are Coming!*?
7) Who plays the Bond girl in *Goldfinger*?
8) *The Birds* is set in what real California town?
9) What 1930s craze is the focus of *They Shoot Horses Don't They*?
10) Who plays the title role in *Alfie*?

Quiz 8 Answers

1) *Torn Curtain*
2) Elmer Gantry

3) Auric – Auric is an adjective meaning of, related to, or containing gold.
4) A heroin filled doll
5) Alistair MacLean
6) Alan Arkin
7) Honor Blackman
8) Bodega Bay
9) Dance marathon
10) Michael Caine

Quiz 9

1) What was Marilyn Monroe's last film?
2) In terms of tickets sold, what is the most popular James Bond film of all time?
3) Who did Sergio Leone originally want to play the lead in *A Fistful of Dollars* but couldn't afford his salary?
4) What movie features a memorable supporting character played by a Hawaiian of Japanese descent who won a silver medal in weightlifting for the U.S. in the 1948 London Olympics and was also a professional wrestler?
5) Who plays Helen Keller in *The Miracle Worker*?
6) What two actresses tied for the 1968 Best Actress Oscar?
7) Scott Wilson and what other actor play the two ex-cons who end up killing a family in a botched robbery in the film *In Cold Blood*?
8) Walt Disney had the second and third highest grossing U.S. films of the 1960s; what are they?
9) What is Joy Adamson's lion cub called in *Born Free*?
10) Who plays the title role in *Gypsy*?

Quiz 9 Answers

1) *The Misfits*
2) *Thunderball*
3) Henry Fonda – Many actors turned down the role before Clint Eastwood accepted and was paid $15,000 for the role.
4) *Goldfinger* – The character of Goldfinger's bodyguard was played by Harold Sakata.
5) Patty Duke
6) Barbra Streisand (*Funny Girl*) and Katharine Hepburn (*The Lion in Winter*)
7) Robert Blake

8) *101 Dalmatians* and *The Jungle Book*
9) Elsa
10) Natalie Wood – portrays stripper Gypsy Rose Lee

Quiz 10

1) In what country were *The Guns of Navarone* located?
2) Who does Michael Caine play in *The Ipcress File*?
3) In *The Italian Job*, what city does the gold heist occur in?
4) What is Norman Bates' hobby in *Psycho*?
5) Who plays the two minstrels in *Cat Ballou* that sing the story?
6) Who plays Queen Guenevere in *Camelot*?
7) Who had their first major acting role in the WWII D-Day Invasion movie *The Longest Day* and also composed the title song for the movie?
8) "The Windmills of Your Mind" is the theme song for what film?
9) What is the name of the computer in *2001: A Space Odyssey*?
10) What was the Beatles' first movie?

Quiz 10 Answers

1) Turkey
2) Harry Palmer
3) Turin, Italy
4) Stuffing birds
5) Nat King Cole and Stubby Kaye
6) Vanessa Redgrave
7) Paul Anka
8) *The Thomas Crown Affair*
9) HAL 9000 – HAL stands for heuristically programmed algorithmic computer.
10) *A Hard Day's Night*

Quiz 11

1) The song "Raindrops Keep Falling on My Head" was introduced in what movie?
2) Besides the cartoon character, what is *The Pink Panther* in the movie of the same name?
3) What movie stars Laurence Olivier as a failing stage performer in an old music hall?
4) For what movie did Rod Steiger win a Best Actor Oscar?

5) The character Marion Crane dies famously in what film?

6) What actors play the unlikely prospecting partners who also share a wife in the singing western *Paint Your Wagon*?

7) What is the name of the young daughter played by Mary Badham in *To Kill a Mockingbird*?

8) What was Elvis Presley's last movie?

9) Who plays the title role in the Best Picture Oscar winner *Oliver!*?

10) What was Clark Gable's last film?

Quiz 11 Answers

1) *Butch Cassidy and the Sundance Kid*
2) Diamond
3) *The Entertainer*
4) *In the Heat of the Night*
5) *Psycho* – shower scene
6) Lee Marvin and Clint Eastwood
7) Scout
8) *Change of Habit* (1969) – with Mary Tyler Moore
9) Mark Lester
10) *The Misfits*

Quiz 12

1) What George Romero zombie flick was released in 1968?

2) *The Good, the Bad and the Ugly* is set during what historical event?

3) The character of the boy Dill Harris who is visiting for the summer in *To Kill a Mockingbird* is based on what real life famous person?

4) In what thriller do Bette Davis and Joan Crawford play sisters?

5) Who plays the title role in *Lawrence of Arabia*?

6) Who made his film debut as Boo Radley in *To Kill a Mockingbird*?

7) Mary Tyler Moore and Julie Andrews live in a hotel for single young ladies in 1920s New York in what movie?

8) Who provides the voice for Baloo the bear in *The Jungle Book*?

9) Who won the Best Director Oscar for *The Graduate*?

10) Who stars in the title role in *Von Ryan's Express*?

Quiz 12 Answers

1) *Night of the Living Dead*
2) U.S. Civil War

3) Truman Capote – He was a childhood friend and neighbor of author Harper Lee, and they remained lifelong friends.
4) *Whatever Happened to Baby Jane*
5) Peter O'Toole
6) Robert Duvall
7) *Thoroughly Modern Millie*
8) Phil Harris
9) Mike Nichols
10) Frank Sinatra

Quiz 13

1) Who plays Tom Robinson who is on trial for rape in *To Kill a Mockingbird*?
2) What Alistair MacLean novel was made into a movie starring Richard Burton and Clint Eastwood?
3) What western stars Henry Fonda, Gregory Peck, John Wayne, Richard Widmark, James Stewart, Spencer Tracy, Walter Brennan, Lee J. Cobb, Karl Malden, Eli Wallach, Robert Preston, Carroll Baker, Carolyn Jones, Debbie Reynolds, and Agnes Moorehead?
4) Who won a Best Supporting Actress Oscar for *Rosemary's Baby*?
5) What pool shark did Jackie Gleason play in *The Hustler*?
6) What is the full name of the character that says, "They call me Mister Tibbs!"?
7) Who plays the young couple drawn into the marital problems of Richard Burton and Elizabeth Taylor's characters in *Who's Afraid of Virginia Woolf*?
8) What comedic western reunited John Wayne and Maureen O'Hara?
9) What comedy has more than 50 stars in it?
10) What character says, "Get your stinking paws off me, you damned dirty ape!"?

Quiz 13 Answers

1) Brock Peters
2) *Where Eagles Dare*
3) *How the West Was Won*
4) Ruth Gordon
5) Minnesota Fats
6) Virgil Tibbs – *In the Heat of the Night*
7) George Segal and Sandy Dennis

8) *McLintock!*
9) *It's a Mad, Mad, Mad, Mad World*
10) George Taylor – played by Charlton Heston in *Planet of the Apes*

Quiz 14

1) What was the nickname of the character played by George Kennedy in *Cool Hand Luke*?
2) Who plays the tunnel king in *The Great Escape*?
3) What was the number one U.S. box office film released in the 1960s?
4) Who plays the Cooler King in *The Great Escape*?
5) What is the name of Dustin Hoffman's character in *Midnight Cowboy*?
6) Who plays Julius Caesar in *Cleopatra*?
7) "Bond. James Bond," is first spoken in what film?
8) In *Bob & Carol & Ted & Alice*, Robert Culp, Natalie Wood, Elliott Gould, and what actress portray the title characters?
9) In *The Absent Minded Professor*, what college is Fred MacMurray a professor at?
10) What two male singers co-star in *State Fair*?

Quiz 14 Answers

1) Dragline
2) Charles Bronson
3) *The Sound of Music* – 1965
4) Steve McQueen
5) Ratso Rizzo
6) Rex Harrison
7) *Dr. No* – Sean Connery
8) Dyan Cannon
9) Medfield College
10) Pat Boone and Bobby Darin

Quiz 15

1) What thriller has a released convict terrorizing a small-town lawyer and his family?
2) What Sam Peckinpah film has an aging group of outlaws looking for one last big score as the traditional American west is disappearing in 1913?
3) Who plays Danny Ocean in *Ocean's 11*?

4) Who co-starred, co-wrote, and directed *Easy Rider*?
5) What three-hour Oscar winning film is set during WWI and the Russian Revolution?
6) What actors play the two opposing lawyers in *Inherit the Wind*?
7) In *Butch Cassidy and the Sundance Kid*, what country does the outlaw pair flee to at the end of the film?
8) In *Bonnie and Clyde*, what are the full names of the title characters?
9) Based on a James Michener novel, what film features Max von Sydow as a missionary and Julie Andrews as his wife?
10) Barbara Parkins, Patty Duke, and Sharon Tate star in a film based on a best-selling novel; it also marked the film debut of Richard Dreyfuss and the first Oscar nomination for composer John Williams; what is the movie?

Quiz 15 Answers

1) *Cape Fear*
2) *The Wild Bunch*
3) Frank Sinatra
4) Dennis Hopper
5) *Doctor Zhivago*
6) Spencer Tracy and Fredric March
7) Bolivia
8) Bonnie Parker and Clyde Barrow
9) *Hawaii*
10) *The Valley of the Dolls*

Quiz 16

1) What was the last Clint Eastwood spaghetti western?
2) What Disney animated feature centers on the King Arthur legend?
3) What is Rooster Cogburn's real name in *True Grit*?
4) What was the most expensive Hollywood film made in the 1960s?
5) What actors star as *The Odd Couple*?
6) What actor is in both *The Magnificent Seven* and *The Dirty Dozen*?
7) In *Irma la Douce*, a former policeman falls in love with a prostitute and tries to get her out of that life by paying for all her time; who plays the prostitute?
8) What film won Katharine Hepburn her third of four Best Actress Oscars?

9) What movie stars Lee Marvin as twins Kid Shelleen and Tim Strawn?

10) What character says, "A boy's best friend is his mother"?

Quiz 16 Answers

1) *The Good, the Bad and the Ugly* – 1966
2) *The Sword in the Stone*
3) Reuben J. Cogburn
4) *Cleopatra* – $31 million at the time
5) Walter Matthau and Jack Lemmon
6) Charles Bronson
7) Shirley MacLaine
8) *The Lion in Winter*
9) *Cat Ballou*
10) Norman Bates – *Psycho*

Quiz 17

1) In *My Fair Lady*, who plays Colonel Pickering who bets Henry Higgins that he can't transform Eliza Doolittle?
2) In *Yours, Mine and Ours*, who plays the widower with 10 children and the widow with 8 children who marry?
3) What Steve McQueen film features some of the most memorable car chase scenes in a Mustang through San Francisco?
4) In *It's a Mad, Mad, Mad, Mad World*, how much money are they chasing after?
5) What actor best known for his 1950s teen television sitcom has a major role in *Cat Ballou*?
6) "Somewhere My Love" is the theme song of what movie?
7) *Alfie* uses an unusual film making technique for its time; what was it?
8) What is the name of the town that is the setting for *The Man Who Shot Liberty Valance*?
9) Who plays Norman Bates in *Psycho*?
10) The Oscar winning movie *Charly* is based on what novel?

Quiz 17 Answers

1) Wilfrid Hyde-White
2) Henry Fonda and Lucille Ball
3) *Bullitt*
4) $350,000

5) Dwayne Hickman – He played Dobie Gillis on television.
6) *Doctor Zhivago*
7) Alfie talks directly to the camera.
8) Shinbone
9) Anthony Perkins
10) *Flowers for Algernon*

Quiz 18

1) What future Best Actress Oscar winner plays the role of Rod Taylor's mother in *The Birds*?
2) In *The Americanization of Emily*, who plays Emily, the English motor pool driver James Garner's character falls in love with?
3) What film stars Paul Newman as a white man raised by Apaches who tries to save the passengers of a stagecoach from bandits?
4) What two famous baseball home run hitters play themselves in *That Touch of Mink*?
5) Who plays Charlie Croker, the brains behind *The Italian Job*?
6) Who plays the captain of the prison camp in *Cool Hand Luke*?
7) What is the name of the character Sidney Poitier plays in *Lilies of the Field*?
8) *Bye Bye Birdie* starring Dick Van Dyke, Janet Leigh, and Ann-Margret is a parody of what celebrity?
9) What movie features the line "You finally really did it. You maniacs! You blew it up!"?
10) Who wrote the novel of the same name on which *Lolita* is based?

Quiz 18 Answers

1) Jessica Tandy
2) Julie Andrews
3) *Hombre*
4) Mickey Mantle and Roger Maris
5) Michael Caine
6) Strother Martin
7) Homer Smith
8) Elvis Presley
9) *Planet of the Apes* – when astronaut George Taylor finds the remnants of the Statue of Liberty
10) Vladimir Nabokov

Quiz 19

1) What did Cool Hand Luke go to jail for?
2) What western won Best Story and Best Song Oscars?
3) Who plays James Bond in *Casino Royale*?
4) Who plays the Texas Ranger La Boeuf in *True Grit*?
5) *Doctor Zhivago* is based on a novel by what author?
6) What racy science fiction movie stars Jane Fonda?
7) *Lawrence of Arabia* is set during WWI; what country are the Arabs united to fight against?
8) What film has the line "Hey! I'm walking here! I'm walking here!"?
9) What movie has the line "What we've got here is a failure to communicate"?
10) Disney's *The Jungle Book* is based on the stories of what author?

Quiz 19 Answers

1) Cutting the heads off parking meters
2) *Butch Cassidy and the Sundance Kid*
3) David Niven
4) Glen Campbell
5) Boris Pasternak
6) *Barbarella*
7) Turkey – Ottoman Empire
8) *Midnight Cowboy* – Dustin Hoffman
9) *Cool Hand Luke* – Strother Martin
10) Rudyard Kipling

Quiz 20

1) What is the name of the character Katharine Ross plays in *Butch Cassidy and the Sundance Kid*?
2) Who plays Yuri Zhivago's love interest Lara in *Doctor Zhivago*?
3) Who plays the title role in *Tom Jones*?
4) What is the name of Goldfinger's bodyguard?
5) What is the name of Audrey Hepburn's character in *Breakfast at Tiffany's*?
6) What movie features Jack Lemmon and Lee Remick as a couple dealing with alcoholism?
7) Who plays the title role in *Lolita*?

8) What town is the setting for *The Music Man*?
9) What was the second of Clint Eastwood's spaghetti westerns directed by Sergio Leone?
10) What is the theme song for *Midnight Cowboy*?

Quiz 20 Answers

1) Etta Place
2) Julie Christie
3) Albert Finney
4) Oddjob
5) Holly Golightly
6) *Days of Wine and Roses*
7) Sue Lyon
8) River City, Iowa
9) *For a Few Dollars More* – 1965
10) "Everybody's Talkin'"

Quiz 21

1) In *Becket*, who plays the title role of Thomas Becket?
2) George Peppard plays Jonas Cord, a young tycoon loosely based on Howard Hughes, in a film based on a Harold Robbins novel; what is the movie?
3) What western features Steve McQueen playing a teen hunting down the killers of his parents?
4) Who directed *Lawrence of Arabia*?
5) What are the names of the two rival gangs in *West Side Story*?
6) What Steve McQueen movie features poker?
7) What film dramatized the Scopes Monkey Trial?
8) What was the first James Bond film to feature the line "A martini. Shaken, not stirred"?
9) Lee Marvin won the Best Actor Oscar for what film?
10) In *Judgement at Nuremberg*, the four people on trial had what role during the Nazi regime?

Quiz 21 Answers

1) Richard Burton
2) *The Carpetbaggers*
3) *Nevada Smith*

4) David Lean
5) Jets and Sharks
6) *The Cincinnati Kid*
7) *Inherit the Wind*
8) *Goldfinger* – Sean Connery
9) *Cat Ballou*
10) Judges

Quiz 22

1) Who plays Fast Eddie Felson's manager in *The Hustler*?
2) What three counties is Eliza Doolittle taught to pronounce in *My Fair Lady*?
3) Katharine Hepburn's real niece plays her daughter in *Guess Who's Coming to Dinner*; who is she?
4) Dean Jones starred in 11 Disney films over his career; what was the first one?
5) What actor says, "We rob banks"?
6) What movie features the line "Plastics" as a desirable future career?
7) Who plays James Bond in *On Her Majesty's Secret Service*?
8) Who wrote the Broadway play and music upon which *The Music Man* is based?
9) In *The Producers*, what is the name of the play they choose to produce with the idea that it is guaranteed to lose money?
10) Who wrote the novel on which *Breakfast at Tiffany's* is based?

Quiz 22 Answers

1) George C. Scott
2) Hertford, Hereford, Hampshire
3) Katharine Houghton
4) *That Darn Cat!*
5) Warren Beatty – *Bonnie and Clyde*
6) *The Graduate*
7) George Lazenby
8) Meredith Wilson
9) *Springtime for Hitler*
10) Truman Capote

1970s

Quiz 1

1) What movie stars Al Pacino as an honest cop who refuses to take bribes and his life is endangered because of it?
2) Who plays the old mountain man, Bear Claw, who teaches Jeremiah Johnson the ways of the mountains in *Jeremiah Johnson*?
3) Who directed *One Flew Over the Cuckoo's Nest*?
4) Who plays the woman involved in the passionate affair in *Last Tango in Paris*?
5) What Disney film stars Barbara Harris and Jodie Foster as a mother and daughter who find themselves occupying each other's bodies?
6) What horror film stars James Brolin and Margot Kidder?
7) What famous director plays the role of Claude LaCombe in *Close Encounters of the Third Kind*?
8) What character does Jackie Gleason play in *Smokey and the Bandit*?
9) What is the name of the con that Paul Newman and Robert Redford carry out in *The Sting*?
10) What is the name of the cannibalistic killer played by Gunnar Hansen in *The Texas Chain Saw Massacre*?

Quiz 1 Answers

1) *Serpico*
2) Will Geer
3) Milos Forman
4) Maria Schneider – She was only 19 at the time.
5) *Freaky Friday*
6) *The Amityville Horror*
7) Francois Truffaut
8) Sheriff Buford T. Justice
9) The wire
10) Leatherface

Quiz 2

1) What movie involves a robbery to get money for a sex change operation?
2) What surrealistic cult classic is set in a post-apocalyptic world and was

directed by David Lynch on a $20,000 budget?
3) Who plays Lois Lane in *Superman*?
4) What was Jamie Lee Curtis' first feature film?
5) In what film does Richard Burton play a psychiatrist trying to discover why a stable boy is harming horses?
6) What is the name of the high school in *Grease*?
7) What adventure film features the characters Daniel Dravot and Peachy Carnehan?
8) In *Monty Python and the Holy Grail*, what did King Arthur and his knights use to defeat the killer rabbit of Caerbannog?
9) Who plays the title role in *Tommy*?
10) What was the first film Clint Eastwood directed?

Quiz 2 Answers

1) *Dog Day Afternoon*
2) *Eraserhead*
3) Margot Kidder
4) *Halloween*
5) *Equus*
6) Rydell
7) *The Man Who Would Be King* – starring Sean Connery and Michael Caine
8) The Holy Hand Grenade of Antioch
9) Roger Daltrey
10) *Play Misty for Me*

Quiz 3

1) What film has a Hollywood composer going through a mid-life crisis and becoming infatuated with a newly married woman half his age?
2) What film has Robert Redford as Sonny Steele, a former rodeo star who steals a thoroughbred horse?
3) What movie has Charles Grodin as a newlywed on his honeymoon who realizes he has made a big mistake and decides he wants a tall blonde played by Cybill Shepherd instead?
4) What is the name of John Travolta's character in *Grease*?
5) What movie has Walter Matthau playing a bank robber who mistakenly steals a very large amount of mob money from a small-town bank?
6) What Woody Allen film has his character becoming president of the country of San Marcos?

7) Who plays the two bumbling outlaws in Disney's *The Apple Dumpling Gang?*

8) What film is based on a novel by James Dickey and was Ned Beatty's screen debut?

9) In *The Shootist*, John Wayne plays a terminally ill gunfighter who gets a room in a boarding house run by a woman and her son; who plays the mother and son?

10) What film stars Michael Caine as Jack Carter, a vicious London gangster investigating the death of his brother?

Quiz 3 Answers

1) *10* – with Dudley Moore and Bo Derek
2) *The Electric Horseman*
3) *The Heartbreak Kid*
4) Danny Zuko
5) *Charley Varrick*
6) *Bananas*
7) Tim Conway and Don Knotts
8) *Deliverance*
9) Lauren Bacall and Ron Howard
10) *Get Carter*

Quiz 4

1) What is the day job of John Travolta's character in *Saturday Night Fever?*
2) Who plays the title roles in *Fun with Dick and Jane?*
3) In what Burt Reynolds film does he play an aging stuntman trying to prove that he's still got what it takes?
4) What film stars Gene Hackman as a paranoid surveillance expert struggling with the morality of his work?
5) What movie is about Hitler's plan to kidnap Winston Churchill?
6) Who won a Best Actress Oscar for *A Touch of Class?*
7) What Best Director Oscar winner appears as an actor in *Chinatown?*
8) What movie has Robert Redford as an unassuming CIA researcher who finds all his colleagues murdered and ends up on the run?
9) What Disney film features David Niven, Jody Foster, and Helen Hayes in her final film appearance?
10) What film includes the famous scene where Jack Nicholson's character tries to order toast which isn't on the menu?

Quiz 4 Answers

1) He works in a paint store.
2) George Segal and Jane Fonda
3) *Hooper*
4) *The Conversation*
5) *The Eagle Has Landed*
6) Glenda Jackson
7) John Huston
8) *Three Days of the Condor*
9) *Candleshoe*
10) *Five Easy Pieces*

Quiz 5

1) In what film is the lead character asked repeatedly "Is it safe?"
2) Who plays the Bond girl in *The Spy Who Loved Me*?
3) Who plays the title role in *The Buddy Holly Story*?
4) What well known actor is listed only as "stud" in the credits for *Myra Breckinridge*?
5) In *The Muppet Movie*, who plays Doc Hopper who wants Kermit as a spokesman for his frog leg restaurant chain?
6) What movie was Mel Gibson's first starring role?
7) Sylvester Stallone was so poor at one point that he sold something he loved for $50 only to buy it back for $3,000 one week later when he sold the script for *Rocky*; what was it?
8) Who plays the investigative reporters Carl Bernstein and Bob Woodward in *All the President's Men*?
9) Who plays Father Merrin, the older priest who performs the exorcism in *The Exorcist*?
10) What film won a Best Actress Oscar for Jane Fonda and a Best Actor Oscar for Jon Voight?

Quiz 5 Answers

1) *Marathon Man* – Laurence Olivier
2) Barbara Bach
3) Gary Busey
4) Tom Selleck
5) Charles Durning

6) *Mad Max*
7) His dog
8) Dustin Hoffman and Robert Redford
9) Max von Sydow
10) *Coming Home*

Quiz 6

1) Who plays the woman Kong goes up one of the World Trade Center towers with in the 1976 remake *King Kong*?
2) What character did Louise Fletcher play in *One Flew over the Cuckoo's Nest*?
3) Who plays the role of Hercule Poirot in *Murder on the Orient Express*?
4) What film stars Edward Albert as a young blind man and Goldie Hawn as his free-spirited neighbor?
5) What film features scenes of the characters playing Russian Roulette?
6) What is the name of Jack Nicholson's character in *Chinatown*?
7) What is the name of the police character played by Roy Scheider in *Jaws*?
8) Who directed *Taxi Driver*?
9) In what state is *Deliverance* set?
10) What Sam Peckinpah film stars Steve McQueen as a recently released convict on the run after a bank robbery goes wrong?

Quiz 6 Answers

1) Jessica Lange
2) Nurse Ratched
3) Albert Finney
4) *Butterflies Are Free*
5) *The Deer Hunter*
6) Jake Gittes
7) Martin Brody
8) Martin Scorsese
9) Georgia - The Cahulawassee River in the book and film is fictional.
10) *The Getaway*

Quiz 7

1) Who spoke the only word in Mel Brooks' *Silent Movie*?
2) What sequel film includes Michael Jackson's first number one solo

song?

3) Who wrote and directed *American Graffiti*?
4) The rock bands Pink Floyd, Led Zeppelin, and Genesis were three of the ten initial investors in what British film?
5) What actor says, "Love means never having to say you're sorry"?
6) What movie has the line "You're gonna need a bigger boat"?
7) What Disney animated feature is about a family of Parisian felines trying to make their way back home?
8) In *Animal House*, what is the name of the college?
9) Who directed the horror thriller *Halloween*?
10) Alex Karras' character famously knocks out a horse in *Blazing Saddles*; what is his character's name?

Quiz 7 Answers

1) Marcel Marceau – French mime
2) *Ben* – It was a sequel to *Willard*; Jackson had a number one hit with the song "Ben".
3) George Lucas
4) *Monty Python and the Holy Grail*
5) Ryan O'Neil
6) *Jaws* – Roy Scheider
7) *The Aristocats*
8) Faber College
9) John Carpenter
10) Mongo

Quiz 8

1) Who plays the young female pitching ace Amanda Whurlitzer in *The Bad News Bears*?
2) What is the name of Robert De Niro's character in *Taxi Driver*?
3) What Wes Craven film is about a family traveling to California who end up in an abandoned military area stalked by violent cannibals?
4) What 1978 film was briefly the highest grossing sequel in history before it was displaced by *Rocky II* the following year?
5) Who plays Dr. Frankenfurter in *The Rocky Horror Picture Show*?
6) *Day of the Jackal* is based on a novel by what author?
7) What was Roger Moore's debut film as James Bond?
8) Who plays the transit police lieutenant who becomes the communicator

between the hijackers and the authorities in *The Taking of Pelham One Two Three*?

9) *The Rose* stars Bette Midler; the film is loosely based on the life of what singer?

10) Who wrote the novel *The Godfather* is based on?

Quiz 8 Answers

1) Tatum O'Neal
2) Travis Bickle
3) *The Hills Have Eyes*
4) *Jaws 2*
5) Tim Curry
6) Frederick Forsyth
7) *Live and Let Die*
8) Walter Matthau
9) Janis Joplin
10) Mario Puzo

Quiz 9

1) What was John Wayne's last movie?
2) In Monty Python's *Life of Brian*, Brian is born at the same time as Jesus but in a different stable and is constantly being mistaken for him; who plays Brian?
3) What former stuntman directed and co-wrote *Smokey and the Bandit*?
4) For what film did Bob Fosse win his only Best Director Oscar?
5) In *Midnight Express*, in what country is the young American imprisoned for smuggling drugs?
6) What is the name of Bill Murray's head camp counselor character in *Meatballs*?
7) In *The Last Detail*, two Navy men are escorting a young man to military prison and decide to show him one last good time; Jack Nicholson plays one of the military escorts; who plays the young prisoner?
8) *Lenny* was about what 1960s comedian?
9) Who plays the reporter after a story in *The Electric Horseman*?
10) What movie stars Bud Cort as a teenager who wants to marry a 79-year-old woman played by Ruth Gordon?

Quiz 9 Answers

1) *The Shootist*
2) Graham Chapman
3) Hal Needham
4) *Cabaret*
5) Turkey
6) Tripper Harrison
7) Randy Quaid
8) Lenny Bruce
9) Jane Fonda
10) *Harold and Maude*

Quiz 10

1) Who plays Robert Thorn in *The Omen*?
2) What disaster film stars Steve McQueen and Paul Newman?
3) What disaster film stars Gene Hackman, Ernest Borgnine, Red Buttons, Roddy McDowall, Stella Stevens, Jack Albertson, and Shelley Winters?
4) *Slap Shot* is about a hapless minor league hockey team; who plays the player/coach of the team?
5) What Sam Peckinpah film stars Dustin Hoffman as young American who moves to rural England with his English wife and gets into a bloody battle with the locals?
6) Grieving after his wife's suicide, a middle-aged American man meets a young French woman and begins a passionate affair without ever revealing their names to each other; what is the film?
7) What is the first name of the possessed girl Linda Blair plays in *The Exorcist*?
8) What two actors play the title roles in *The In-Laws*?
9) *Breaking Away* is about a small-town teen obsessed with cycling and the Italian cycling team; in what real town is the movie set?
10) What two real life singers co-star in *A Star is Born*?

Quiz 10 Answers

1) Gregory Peck
2) *The Towering Inferno*
3) *The Poseidon Adventure*
4) Paul Newman
5) *Straw Dogs*

6) *Last Tango in Paris*
7) Regan
8) Peter Falk and Alan Arkin
9) Bloomington, Indiana – home of Indiana University
10) Barbra Streisand and Kris Kristofferson

Quiz 11

1) What film is based on the life of its director Bob Fosse?
2) Who plays the rookie female partner teamed with Harry Callahan in *The Enforcer*?
3) What female singing star has a starring role in Disney's *Pete's Dragon*?
4) "Attica! Attica! Attica! Attica!" is from what movie?
5) In *Breaking Away*, what name do the university students call the locals and is also the name the local teens use for their cycling team in the big race?
6) In *Star Wars*, what is the name of Princess Leia's home planet?
7) For what film did Art Carney win a Best Actor Oscar?
8) What film has con man Moses Pray taking on nine-year-old Addie Loggins as his partner?
9) What does China syndrome refer to in *The China Syndrome*?
10) What movie features the line "You've got to ask yourself one question: 'Do I feel lucky?' Well do ya, punk?"

Quiz 11 Answers

1) *All That Jazz*
2) Tyne Daly
3) Helen Reddy
4) *Dog Day Afternoon* – Al Pacino
5) Cutters – Many of the middle-aged locals had worked in the limestone quarry cutting stone.
6) Alderaan
7) *Harry and Tonto*
8) *Paper Moon*
9) A hypothetical catastrophic failure where a nuclear reactor melts through the floor of its containment system and penetrates the earth's surface as if traveling through toward China.
10) *Dirty Harry*

Quiz 12

1) Who plays Frankenstein's fiancé in *Young Frankenstein*?
2) In *Heaven Can Wait*, James Mason plays the angel trying to help Warren Beatty find a new body; what is his character's name?
3) What was the most expensive Hollywood film made in the 1970s?
4) What was the sequel to *True Grit*?
5) What film has the insult "Your mother was a hamster, and your father smelt of elderberries"?
6) Who plays the Bond girl Solitaire, a tarot card reader, in *Live and Let Die*?
7) What WWII movie won seven Oscars including Best Picture, Best Actor, and Best Director?
8) Marvin Hamlisch created the music for *The Sting*; much of the score is based on the work of what ragtime era composer?
9) For what film did Jane Fonda win her first Oscar?
10) What is the theme song for *M*A*S*H*?

Quiz 12 Answers

1) Madeline Kahn
2) Mr. Jordan
3) *Superman* – $55 million at the time
4) *Rooster Cogburn*
5) *Monty Python and the Holy Grail*
6) Jane Seymour
7) *Patton*
8) Scott Joplin
9) *Klute*
10) "Suicide is Painless"

Quiz 13

1) What medical thriller is based on a novel by Robin Cook and stars Genevieve Bujold and Michael Douglas?
2) What is the name of the summer camp in *Meatballs*?
3) What film has the line "Keep your friends close, but your enemies closer"?
4) What Neil Simon story finds Paula and her daughter forced to live with struggling actor Elliot?
5) Who plays Vito Corleone's two sons in *The Godfather*?

6) What actor is stung in *The Sting*?

7) What Martin Scorsese film stars Robert De Niro and Harvey Keitel in a mob related story?

8) What was Bruce Lee's final film?

9) *Willard* is about a social misfit who uses his pet rats to get revenge; who plays the title role?

10) In *Willy Wonka and the Chocolate Factory*, what is the last name of the protagonist Charlie?

Quiz 13 Answers

1) *Coma*

2) Camp North Star

3) *The Godfather: Part II* – Al Pacino

4) *The Goodbye Girl*

5) Al Pacino and James Caan

6) Robert Shaw

7) *Mean Streets*

8) *Enter the Dragon*

9) Bruce Davison

10) Bucket

Quiz 14

1) What is the name of Gene Hackman's character in *The French Connection*?

2) What two actors play Superman's Krypton father and Earth father in *Superman*?

3) What is the classical piece of music that is playing while Dudley Moore and Bo Derek are making love in *10*?

4) Who plays the role of Tevye in *Fiddler on the Roof*?

5) What Marlon Brando film was widely banned?

6) In *Animal House*, John Vernon plays the dean who is out to get the Deltas; what is the dean's name?

7) What disaster film stars Charlton Heston, Ava Gardner, George Kennedy, Lorne Greene, Genevieve Bujold, Richard Roundtree, Barry Sullivan, Lloyd Nolan, and Walter Matthau?

8) Who directed *Alien*?

9) In *Star Wars Episode IV – A New Hope*, who plays the role of Chewbacca?

10) In *Oh, God!*, who plays the assistant manager of a grocery store that God talks to?

Quiz 14 Answers

1) Popeye Doyle
2) Marlon Brando as Jor-El and Glenn Ford as Jonathan Kent
3) *Bolero* – by Maurice Ravel
4) Topol
5) *Last Tango in Paris*
6) Dean Vernon Wormer
7) *Earthquake*
8) Ridley Scott
9) Peter Mayhew – He is 7'3" tall.
10) John Denver

Quiz 15

1) What is the name of Sigourney Weaver's character in *Alien*?
2) What movie was inspired by actual events surrounding water rights in California in the 1920s?
3) Who plays Al Pacino's lover in *Dog Day Afternoon*?
4) What Barbra Streisand song won the Best Original Song Oscar for *A Star is Born*?
5) What film has news anchorman Howard Beale threatening to kill himself on live television after learning he is being forced to retire?
6) Who plays Joanna Eberhart who moves to Stepford in *The Stepford Wives*?
7) What is the name of the serial killer in *Halloween*?
8) *Bound for Glory* portrays the early life of what real person?
9) What is the name of the Tennessee sheriff Joe Don Baker plays in *Walking Tall*?
10) What film pairs Gene Wilder and Richard Pryor on a train?

Quiz 15 Answers

1) Ellen Ripley
2) *Chinatown*
3) Chris Sarandon
4) "Evergreen"
5) *Network*
6) Katharine Ross
7) Michael Myers

8) Woody Guthrie
9) Buford Pusser
10) *Silver Streak*

Quiz 16

1) What film features the line "Love means never having to say you're sorry"?
2) Who is the first character to speak in *Star Wars*?
3) In what city is *Cabaret* set?
4) In *The Jerk*, what is the name of Steve Martin's idiot character?
5) What film was Sean Connery's last James Bond role for 12 years?
6) In *Day of the Jackal*, the Jackal is trying to kill French president Charles de Gaulle and disguises his rifle as what to get past the police?
7) What are the first names of the characters played by Ryan O'Neal and Ali MacGraw in *Love Story*?
8) *Lady Sings the Blues* is about the life and music career of what jazz singer?
9) Clint Eastwood plays trucker turned prize-fighter Philo Beddoe in *Every Which Way But Loose*; what is the name of his pet orangutan?
10) What film stars Warren Beatty, Julie Christie, and Goldie Hawn and was also Carrie Fisher's screen debut?

Quiz 16 Answers

1) *Love Story*
2) C-3PO
3) Berlin – in 1931 before the rise of Hitler
4) Navin Johnson
5) *Diamonds Are Forever*
6) Crutches
7) Oliver and Jenny
8) Billie Holiday
9) Clyde
10) *Shampoo*

Quiz 17

1) Walter Matthau plays a former minor league baseball player coaching a team of little league misfits in *The Bad News Bears*; what is his character's name?

2) Who are the four actors who play the friends on a canoe trip in *Deliverance*?

3) What two future cast members of television's *Taxi* sitcom appear in *One Flew Over the Cuckoo's Nest*?

4) What was the second Monty Python film after *Monty Python and the Holy Grail*?

5) Who reprises his role as Tom Hagen, the consigliere to the Corleone family, in *The Godfather Part II*?

6) In *Heaven Can Wait*, Warren Beatty plays Joe Pendleton who through a heavenly mistake is taken too early and must find a suitable new body; what did Joe Pendleton do for a living?

7) Gene Wilder plays a gunslinger in *Blazing Saddles*; he is known as Jim and by what other name?

8) Who did Gregory Peck portray in *The Boys from Brazil*?

9) Laurence Olivier plays a famous villain in *Marathon Man*; what is the name of his character?

10) Who directed and starred in *The Gauntlet*?

Quiz 17 Answers

1) Morris Buttermaker

2) Burt Reynolds, Jon Voight, Ned Beatty, Ronny Cox

3) Danny DeVito and Christopher Lloyd – It was the film debut of Christopher Lloyd.

4) *Life of Brian*

5) Robert Duvall

6) Quarterback for the Los Angeles Rams

7) The Waco Kid

8) Dr. Josef Mengele

9) Dr. Christian Szell – also known as the White Angel of Auschwitz

10) Clint Eastwood

Quiz 18

1) Who won the only acting Oscar for *Annie Hall*?

2) Who dubbed Miss Piggy's singing voice in *The Muppet Movie*?

3) Based on a true story, what movie features bank robber Frank Morris masterminding a feat that had never been accomplished before?

4) What was the top grossing Walt Disney movie of the 1970s?

5) What is the name of Charles Bronson's character in *Death Wish*?

6) What science fiction movie features a seemingly idyllic world with the

catch that your life must end at age 30?

7) In *Harry and Tonto*, Art Carney plays Harry; who or what is Tonto?

8) In *Willy Wonka and the Chocolate Factory*, what is the name of the candy that Charlie returns at the end to prove he is worthy of taking over everything?

9) What is the name of the fictional resort town in *Jaws*?

10) What city is the setting for *Chinatown*?

Quiz 18 Answers

1) Diane Keaton – best actress
2) Johnny Mathis
3) *Escape from Alcatraz* – It was the only escape ever from Alcatraz.
4) *The Rescuers*
5) Paul Kersey
6) *Logan's Run*
7) A cat – Tonto is Harry's cat.
8) Everlasting Gobstopper
9) Amity Island
10) Los Angeles

Quiz 19

1) What movie stars Edward Woodward as a policeman lured to a remote Scottish island for a pagan sacrifice?

2) In *Close Encounters of the Third Kind*, what is the real location that Richard Dreyfuss' character builds in mashed potatoes and is drawn to?

3) What is the name of John Travolta's character in *Saturday Night Fever*?

4) What actor had his film debut in *Animal House* as Chip Diller?

5) Who are the two stars in *Sleuth*?

6) What was the first *Star Trek* movie?

7) "I'm going to make him an offer he can't refuse," is from what film?

8) In Disney's animated feature *The Rescuers*, who provides the voices for the two mice searching for the kidnapped girl?

9) Who plays the robotic gunslinger turned killer in *Westworld*?

10) Who plays the title role of the former Green Beret who saves wild horses from being slaughtered in *Billy Jack*?

Quiz 19 Answers

1) *The Wicker Man*

2) Devils Tower National Monument in Wyoming
3) Tony Manero
4) Kevin Bacon
5) Laurence Olivier and Michael Caine
6) *Star Trek: The Motion Picture* – 1979
7) *The Godfather* – Marlon Brando
8) Eva Gabor and Bob Newhart
9) Yul Brynner
10) Tom Laughlin

Quiz 20

1) In the first of what would be multiple films, what film features a stray dog saving two kidnapped children?
2) In *Eyes of Laura Mars*, a fashion photographer develops the ability to see through the eyes of a serial killer; who plays the title role?
3) What are the names of the rival gangs in *Grease*?
4) Who directed *M*A*S*H*?
5) What two actors play Peter and John, the two friends who take a vacation to *Westworld*?
6) What two actresses play the two women whose lives are dedicated to ballet in *The Turning Point*?
7) What Woody Allen film has a middle-aged divorced television writer dating a teenage girl and falling in love with his best friend's mistress?
8) What was the first of the big production 1970s disaster genre films?
9) What was the sequel to *Billy Jack*?
10) Where is the prison in *Pappillon*?

Quiz 20 Answers

1) *Benji*
2) Faye Dunaway
3) Thunderbirds and Scorpions
4) Robert Altman
5) Richard Benjamin and James Brolin
6) Anne Bancroft and Shirley MacLaine
7) *Manhattan*
8) *Airport* – starring Burt Lancaster and Dean Martin
9) *The Trial of Billy Jack*
10) French Guiana – Devil's Island

Quiz 21

1) What Alfred Hitchcock film centers on a serial killer who is strangling women with a necktie?

2) Henri Charriere is a convicted murderer serving a prison sentence; he is better known by his nickname which is also the title of the film; what is it?

3) *Monty Python and the Holy Grail* has imaginary horses because they didn't have the budget for real horses; what is used to simulate the sounds of horses' hooves clopping?

4) In *Blazing Saddles*, the people in the town of Rock Ridge all have the same last name; what is it?

5) Meryl Streep and Dustin Hoffman play husband and wife in what movie?

6) Who provides the demon's voice for Linda Blair's performance in *The Exorcist*?

7) What film is about a gang leader who goes on a violent spree and is captured and undergoes aversion therapy?

8) What actor says, "I love the smell of napalm in the morning"?

9) In *Jaws*, Quint describes the sinking of a ship during WWII and how the sharks attacked the survivors. His story is based on a real event; what is the name of the ship that sank?

10) Who won a Best Actor Oscar for *Network*?

Quiz 21 Answers

1) *Frenzy*
2) *Papillon*
3) Coconut halves clapped together
4) Johnson
5) *Kramer vs Kramer*
6) Mercedes McCambridge
7) *A Clockwork Orange*
8) Robert Duvall - *Apocalypse Now*
9) *USS Indianapolis* – After four days in the water, only 317 of the original 1,196-man crew were rescued. It is the U.S. Navy's single worst loss at sea and the worst shark attack in recorded history.
10) Peter Finch

Quiz 22

1) Who plays the metal-toothed Jaws character in the James Bond film *Moonraker*?

2) What Francis Ford Coppola film stars Martin Sheen, Marlon Brando, Robert Duvall, Laurence Fishburne, Dennis Hopper, and Harrison Ford?

3) What was the number one U.S. box office film released in the 1970s?

4) Based on a Richard Adam's novel, what animated feature follows a group of rabbits looking for a new place to live?

5) "I'm mad as hell, and I'm not going to take this anymore!" is a line from what movie?

6) What area of the world do Michael Caine and Sean Connery's characters become kings of in *The Man Who Would Be King*?

7) What comedy centers on two football players and their mutual girlfriend?

8) What is Carrie's last name in *Carrie*?

9) What film has the quote "You talkin' to me?"

10) What WWII movie stars Laurence Olivier, Sean Connery, Anthony Hopkins, Michael Caine, Gene Hackman, Robert Redford, James Caan, Elliott Gould, Maximilian Schell, Dirk Bogarde, and Ryan O'Neal?

Quiz 22 Answers

1) Richard Kiel – Kiel was 7'2" tall.

2) *Apocalypse Now*

3) *Star Wars* – 1977

4) *Watership Down*

5) *Network* – Peter Finch

6) Kafiristan – eastern Afghanistan

7) *Semi-Tough*

8) White

9) *Taxi Driver* – Robert DeNiro

10) *A Bridge Too Far*

1980s

Quiz 1

1) Who plays the young Amish boy who witnesses a murder and is protected by Harrison Ford in *Witness*?

2) What film features two young Australian sprinters who face the brutal realities of war when they are sent to fight in Turkey during WWI?

3) Why wasn't the original *Tron* movie considered for a visual effects Oscar?

4) What movie is about six guests invited to a strange house who must solve a murder mystery?

5) In *Risky Business*, who plays the prostitute Lana that Tom Cruise's character falls for?

6) In *Stand and Deliver*, who plays the teacher in a tough high school who inspires his students to learn calculus?

7) How many *Rocky* movies were there in the 1980s?

8) What film starring Helen Bonham Carter as a young Englishwoman visiting Florence is based on an E.M. Forster novel?

9) What actor says, "You fell victim to one of the classic blunders - the most famous of which is never get involved in a land war in Asia - but only slightly less well-known is this: Never go in against a Sicilian when death is on the line"?

10) Who plays the title role of male escort Julian Kaye in *American Gigolo*?

Quiz 1 Answers

1) Lukas Haas
2) *Gallipoli*
3) The Academy felt the filmmakers had cheated by using computers.
4) *Clue*
5) Rebecca De Mornay
6) Edward James Olmos
7) Two – *Rocky III* and *Rocky IV*
8) *A Room with a View*
9) Wallace Shawn – as Vizzini in *The Princess Bride*
10) Richard Gere

Quiz 2

1) What comedy has the tagline Say it once... Say it twice... But we dare you to say it THREE TIMES"?

2) What film won the most Oscars in the 1980s?

3) Who plays the two male leads in *Dirty Rotten Scoundrels*?

4) In *Big*, what song do they play by dancing on the giant piano keyboard on the floor?

5) How many 1980s films were brother and sister John and Joan Cusack in together?

6) Linda Hunt won an Oscar for *The Year of Living Dangerously*; it was the first Oscar for what?

7) Robert De Niro plays bounty hunter Jack Walsh who is chasing a bail jumping mob accountant in *Midnight Run*; who plays the accountant?

8) What 1932 violent classic starring Paul Muni was remade with Al Pacino in the starring role in 1983?

9) What movie is based on the true story of Christy Brown who was born with cerebral palsy and went on to become a writer and painter?

10) Who plays the girl in the famous pool scene from *Fast Times at Ridgemont High*?

Quiz 2 Answers

1) *Beetlejuice*

2) *The Last Emperor* – nine Oscars

3) Michael Caine and Steve Martin

4) "Heart and Soul" – by Hoagy Carmichael

5) Five – *Class* (1983), *Sixteen Candles* (1984), *Grandview USA* (1984), *Broadcast News* (1987), *Say Anything...* (1989)

6) Playing the opposite sex

7) Charles Grodin

8) *Scarface*

9) *My Left Foot*

10) Phoebe Cates

Quiz 3

1) What movie about a cop trying to stop a killer cult stars Sylvester Stallone and his then real-life wife Brigitte Nielsen?

2) What film tells the story of John Merrick, a real 19th century English man?

3) What four actors play the title roles in *Ghostbusters*?
4) What film is set during the Khmer Rouge reign in Cambodia and won Haing S. Ngor a Best Supporting Actor Oscar?
5) What is the title of the sequel to *Romancing the Stone*?
6) In *Gandhi*, what country is Gandhi in when he is thrown off a train for being Indian and starts his non-violent civil rights campaign?
7) What Oliver Stone movie won Best Picture and Best Director Oscars?
8) What Jim Henson and Frank Oz film features a Gelfing on a quest?
9) What romantic comedy has the tagline "Can men and women be friends or does sex always get in the way?"
10) What movie has Sean Connery in the role of Juan Sanchez Villa-Lobos Ramirez?

Quiz 3 Answers

1) *Cobra*
2) *The Elephant Man*
3) Bill Murray, Dan Aykroyd, Harold Ramis, Ernie Hudson
4) *The Killing Fields*
5) *The Jewel of the Nile*
6) South Africa – After winning recognition for the rights of Indians in South Africa, he was invited back to India and took up the fight for India's independence from British rule.
7) *Platoon*
8) *The Dark Crystal*
9) *When Harry Met Sally*
10) *Highlander*

Quiz 4

1) Kevin Kline won a Best Supporting Actor Oscar for what film?
2) Who plays the title role in *An American Werewolf in London*?
3) What is the name of Michael Douglas' character in *Wall Street*?
4) In *The Blue Lagoon*, Brooke Shields plays the young woman stranded on the island; who plays the young man?
5) Sally Field won a Best Actress Oscar for her portrayal of a single woman trying to survive on a small farm during the Great Depression; what is the film?
6) Who plays the brothers Mikey and Brandon Walsh who along with their friends set out to find a pirate treasure in *The Goonies*?
7) What movie features a single mother and a boy with craniodiaphyseal

dysplasia?

8) In *Gorillas in the Mist*, Sigourney Weaver stars as what real-life scientist who went to Africa to study the vanishing mountain gorillas and fought to protect them?

9) Who plays the title role in *The Last Temptation of Christ*?

10) "Listen to me, mister. You're my knight in shining armor. Don't you forget it. You're going to get back on that horse, and I'm going to be right behind you, holding on tight, and away we're gonna go, go, go!" is from what movie?

Quiz 4 Answers

1) *A Fish Called Wanda*
2) David Naughton
3) Gordon Gekko
4) Christopher Atkins
5) *Places in the Heart*
6) Sean Astin and Josh Brolin
7) *Mask*
8) Dian Fossey
9) Willem Dafoe
10) *On Golden Pond* – Katharine Hepburn

Quiz 5

1) What comedy features a house destroyed by popcorn?

2) What film has s troubled boy drawn into the mythical land of Fantasia through a book?

3) In *Good Morning Vietnam*, Robin Williams' character is based on a real-life disc jockey on U.S. Armed Forces Radio in Saigon during the Vietnam War; what is his name?

4) Who plays Miss Hannigan in *Annie*?

5) In *The Mission*, Jeremy Irons plays a Spanish Jesuit priest who goes into the South American wilderness in the 18th century to build a mission; who plays the slave trader who is initially an opponent but converts over to his side?

6) What was Clint Eastwood's sequel to *Every Which Way But Loose*?

7) What South African film features a bushman in the Kalahari Desert who discovers a Coke bottle?

8) What comedy has the tagline "Bill Murray is back among the ghosts. Only this time, it's three against one"?

9) Who was the first choice to play Indiana Jones but missed out due to other commitments?

10) What is the name of Bill Murray's character in *Ghostbusters*?

Quiz 5 Answers

1) *Real Genius*
2) *The NeverEnding Story*
3) Adrian Cronauer
4) Carol Burnett
5) Robert De Niro
6) *Any Which Way You Can*
7) *The Gods Must Be Crazy*
8) *Scrooged* – alternative remake of *A Christmas Carol*
9) Tom Selleck
10) Peter Venkman

Quiz 6

1) *A Christmas Story* is based on what writer's work?
2) A young English boy struggles to survive under Japanese occupation during WWII in what film?
3) In *Do the Right Thing*, what is the name of the character Spike Lee plays?
4) What film is based on the Stephen King novella *The Body*?
5) Jodie Foster stars with Kelly McGillis in what movie that won Foster her first Best Actress Oscar?
6) William Hurt won a Best Actor Oscar for his role as one of two men sharing a prison cell in Argentina in what movie?
7) Where is John Carpenter's *The Thing* starring Kurt Russell set?
8) In *All the Right Moves*, Tom Cruise plays a high school football player after a football scholarship; who plays his coach he clashes with?
9) What actors play the mother and father in *A Christmas Story*?
10) Who are the two actors who get stuck traveling together in *Planes, Trains and Automobiles*?

Quiz 6 Answers

1) Jean Shepherd
2) *Empire of the Sun* – Christian Bale plays the boy; he was 13 at the time.
3) Mookie
4) *Stand by Me*

5) *The Accused*
6) *Kiss of the Spider Woman*
7) Antarctica
8) Craig T. Nelson
9) Melinda Dillon and Darren McGavin
10) Steve Martin and John Candy

Quiz 7

1) What comedy has the tagline "Only their mother can tell them apart"?
2) What was the first film where Eddie Murphy plays multiple characters in the same movie?
3) What role did F. Murray Abraham play in *Amadeus*?
4) "Nobody puts Baby in a corner," is from what movie?
5) What movie starring Shirley MacLaine, Debra Winger and Jack Nicholson won Best Picture, Director, Actress, and Supporting Actor Oscars?
6) Jack Nicholson and Meryl Streep co-star in a story about an alcoholic drifter who spends Halloween in his home town after being away for decades; what is the film?
7) What movie features the line "Here's Johnny!"?
8) What is the name of the terrorist thief played by Alan Rickman in *Die Hard*?
9) What science fiction thriller stars Harrison Ford, Rutger Hauer, Sean Young and Daryl Hannah?
10) What is Eddie Murphy's character name in *Beverly Hills Cop*?

Quiz 7 Answers

1) *Twins* – starring Arnold Schwarzenegger and Danny DeVito
2) *Coming to America* – Murphy plays four characters.
3) Antonio Salieri
4) *Dirty Dancing* – Patrick Swayze
5) *Terms of Endearment*
6) *Ironweed*
7) *The Shining* – Jack Nicholson
8) Hans Gruber
9) *Blade Runner*
10) Axel Foley

Quiz 8

1) Who won a Best Actor Oscar for *Amadeus*?
2) Set in a Los Angeles office building, the 1979 novel *Nothing Lasts Forever* is the basis for what film?
3) In *Stir Crazy*, what talent does Gene Wilder's character have that makes him popular with the prison warden?
4) What Steven Soderbergh film stars Andie MacDowell and James Spader in a tale of voyeurism?
5) In *Urban Cowboy*, what it the name of the real-life nightclub they hang out at and ride the mechanical bull?
6) What science fiction film has real life married couple Hume Cronyn and Jessica Tandy playing a married couple and won Don Ameche a Best Supporting Actor Oscar?
7) What was the last feature film Ingmar Bergman directed?
8) What character says, "If you build it, he will come"?
9) For what movie did Paul Newman win his only acting Oscar?
10) What film has Paul Newman as a down and out Boston lawyer who takes a medical malpractice suit to trial?

Quiz 8 Answers

1) F. Murray Abraham
2) *Die Hard*
3) Bronc riding
4) *Sex, Lies and Videotape*
5) Gilley's – At the time, it was the largest nightclub in the world.
6) *Cocoon*
7) *Fanny and Alexander*
8) Shoeless Joe Jackson – played by Ray Liotta in *Field of Dreams*
9) *The Color of Money*
10) *The Verdict*

Quiz 9

1) In *The Terminator*, what is the name of the future system that became self-aware and tried to wipe out all humans?
2) After an apocalypse, two Valley Girls are left to fight against cannibal zombies; what is the film?
3) In the cult classic *Repo Man*, who plays the young punk rocker Otto?
4) What Terry Gilliam film is set in a retro futuristic world and stars

Jonathan Pryce and Robert De Niro?

5) What movie series had the most sequel releases in the 1980s?

6) What film has the tagline "The story of eight old friends searching for something they lost, and finding that all they needed was each other"?

7) What film is the story of two FBI agents sent to investigate the disappearance of three young civil rights activists during the 1960s?

8) What film has the tagline "May the Schwartz be with you!"?

9) What movie is about the Mercury astronauts and stars Ed Harris, Scott Glenn, Sam Shepard, Barbara Hershey and Dennis Quaid?

10) Who directed *A Room with a View*, *Howards End*, and *The Remains of the Day*?

Quiz 9 Answers

1) Skynet
2) *Night of the Comet*
3) Emilio Estevez
4) *Brazil*
5) *Halloween* – Four sequels were released in the 1980s.
6) *The Big Chill*
7) *Mississippi Burning*
8) *Spaceballs*
9) *The Right Stuff*
10) James Ivory

Quiz 10

1) What famous actor made his film debut in *A Nightmare on Elm Street*?

2) What movie is based on Philip K. Dick's book *Do Androids Dream of Electric Sheep*?

3) What comedy has the tagline "It's the story of a man, a woman, and a rabbit in a triangle of trouble"?

4) Who plays The Joker in *Batman*?

5) Contractually, who had to be first offered the role of John McClane in *Die Hard*?

6) What Oscar winning actress says, "Snap out of it!"?

7) The first film Steven Spielberg produced was a horror film which he also co-wrote; it starred Craig T. Nelson and JoBeth Williams; what is the movie?

8) Who plays Gene Hackman's love interest in *Hoosiers*?

9) What song in *Arthur* won an Oscar?

10) In *Stand by Me*, what four child actors who all went on to significant acting careers play the 12-year-old friends Gordy, Chris, Teddy, and Vern who go looking for the dead body?

Quiz 10 Answers

1) Johnny Depp
2) *Blade Runner*
3) *Who Framed Roger Rabbit*
4) Jack Nicholson
5) Frank Sinatra – He was 73 at the time. The movie is based on the book *Nothing Lasts Forever* which was a sequel to *The Detective* which had been made into a movie in 1968 starring Sinatra; contractually, he had to be offered the role first.
6) Cher – *Moonstruck*
7) *Poltergeist*
8) Barbara Hershey
9) "Best That You Can Do"
10) Will Wheaton, River Phoenix, Corey Feldman, Jerry O'Connell

Quiz 11

1) In *The Breakfast Club*, five high school students meet in Saturday detention; who are the five actors who play the students?
2) *A Passage to India* is set in the 1920s and is based on a novel by what author?
3) In *Bull Durham*, Kevin Costner plays an aging catcher, and Tim Robbins plays an up and coming young pitcher; who plays the woman who gets romantically involved with both?
4) What character says, "Cinderella story. Outta nowhere. A former greenskeeper, now, about to become the Masters champion. It looks like a mirac... It's in the hole! It's in the hole! It's in the hole!"?
5) What was the top grossing animated film of the 1980s in the U.S.?
6) What film followed the career of athletes Eric Henry Liddell and Harold Abrahams?
7) What Terry Gilliam film has a young boy accidentally joining a group of time traveling dwarfs looking for treasure to steal?
8) What romantic comedy has the line "I'll have what she's having"?
9) Who plays Reverend Shaw Moore, the minister behind the dancing ban in *Footloose*?

10) What is the name of the character Dustin Hoffman plays in *Rain Man*?

Quiz 11 Answers

1) Molly Ringwald, Judd Nelson, Anthony Michael Hall, Emilio Estevez, Ally Sheedy
2) E.M. Forster
3) Susan Sarandon
4) Carl Spackler – played by Bill Murray in *Caddyshack*
5) *The Little Mermaid*
6) *Chariots of Fire*
7) *Time Bandits*
8) *When Harry Met Sally* – Meg Ryan's fake orgasm scene in the restaurant
9) John Lithgow
10) Raymond Babbitt

Quiz 12

1) Who directed, wrote the screenplay, and plays the title role in *Henry V*?
2) In what country is the action adventure comedy *Romancing the Stone* set?
3) What film directed by Jean-Jacques Annaud doesn't contain a single word of any modern language and traces the movements of a tribe of pre-historic humans?
4) What is the name of Sean Penn's character in *Fast Times at Ridgemont High*?
5) In *Gremlins*, the cute, furry creature Gizmo is what kind of animal?
6) In *Conan the Destroyer*, what sports legend appears along with Arnold Schwarzenegger?
7) What was the last of the five *Dirty Harry* movies?
8) Who plays the woman created by two unpopular teenagers in *Weird Science*?
9) Who plays Mozart in *Amadeus*?
10) What Sam Raimi film has five college students spending time in a remote cabin and unleashing evil and features the debut of Bruce Campbell's Ash character?

Quiz 12 Answers

1) Kenneth Branagh
2) Colombia – Ironically, the story centers around an American

kidnapping in Colombia, but an increase in American kidnappings in Colombia caused the filming to be moved to Mexico.

3) *Quest for Fire*
4) Jeff Spicoli
5) Mogwai
6) Wilt Chamberlain
7) *The Dead Pool*
8) Kelly LeBrock
9) Tom Hulce
10) *The Evil Dead*

Quiz 13

1) In *Back to the Future*, what year does Marty McFly go back to?
2) Who plays the mother and father of the family dealing with the accidental death of its oldest son in *Ordinary People*?
3) In *Uncle Buck*, John Candy plays the title role of an idle, slob bachelor who agrees to watch over his brother's kids; who plays his young nephew?
4) What comedy ends with the line "Hey, can I try on your yellow dress?"
5) In *Stripes*, who plays Bill Murray's best friend that he convinces to enlist in the army?
6) In what film did Sean Connery play James Bond after a 12-year absence?
7) What film stars Burt Lancaster as an aging small-time gangster and was nominated for all five of the major Oscars?
8) Who plays Daniel LaRusso's romantic interest in *The Karate Kid*?
9) What model of car is *Christine*?
10) "They only met once, but it changed their lives forever," is the tagline for what teen movie?

Quiz 13 Answers

1) 1955
2) Mary Tyler Moore and Donald Sutherland
3) Macaulay Culkin
4) *Tootsie*
5) Harold Ramis
6) *Never Say Never Again*
7) *Atlantic City*

8) Elisabeth Shue
9) Plymouth Fury
10) *The Breakfast Club*

Quiz 14

1) In *Airplane*, what older actress says, "Chump don' want no help, Chump don' git no help!"?
2) In *Cocktail*, who plays Tom Cruise's bartending mentor?
3) What film features the line "Go ahead, make my day"?
4) In the *Lethal Weapon* movies, what is Mel Gibson's character name?
5) The Japanese film *Ran* is based in part on Shakespeare's King Lear and was one of the last films of what Japanese director?
6) Who directed *Das Boot* about a German U-boat during WWII?
7) What was the most expensive Hollywood film made during the 1980s?
8) What Rob Reiner film is a mockumentary of a British rock band?
9) What movie was Julia Roberts' first starring role and also Matt Damon's film debut?
10) What was Sergio Leone's last film and stars Robert De Niro and James Woods as Jewish gangsters in New York?

Quiz 14 Answers

1) Barbara Billingsley – June Cleaver from *Leave it to Beaver*
2) Bryan Brown
3) *Sudden Impact* – Clint Eastwood
4) Martin Riggs
5) Akira Kurosawa – also directed *The Seven Samurai*, *Rashomon*, *Yojimbo*
6) Wolfgang Petersen
7) *Who Framed Roger Rabbit* - $70 million at the time
8) *This Is Spinal Tap*
9) *Mystic Pizza*
10) *Once Upon a Time in America*

Quiz 15

1) What comedy has the line "I was a better man with you as a woman than I ever was with a woman as a man. Know what I mean?"
2) What Best Picture and Best Director Oscar winning film has the tagline "He was the Lord of Ten Thousand Years, the absolute monarch of China. He was born to rule a world of ancient tradition. Nothing

prepared him for our world of change"?

3) What film starring Kathleen Turner and Nicolas Cage has the tagline "Knowing what you know now, what would you do differently?"

4) What movie stars Sally Field, Dolly Parton, Shirley MacLaine, Daryl Hannah, Olympia Dukakis, and Julia Roberts in a small Louisiana town?

5) What film has Loretta Castorini, a bookkeeper from Brooklyn, falling in love with the brother of the man she has agreed to marry?

6) What are the nicknames of flying partners Tom Cruise and Anthony Edwards in *Top Gun*?

7) What was James Cameron's first film as a director?

8) In *E.T. the Extra-Terrestrial*, what is E.T.'s candy of choice?

9) What was Robin Williams first starring film?

10) In *The Shining*, novelist Jack Torrance played by Jack Nicholson takes a job as caretaker at a hotel where an evil presence drives him crazy; what is the name of the hotel?

Quiz 15 Answers

1) *Tootsie*
2) *The Last Emperor*
3) *Peggy Sue Got Married*
4) *Steel Magnolias*
5) *Moonstruck*
6) Maverick and Goose
7) *The Terminator* – 1984
8) Reese's Pieces
9) *Popeye*
10) Overlook Hotel

Quiz 16

1) What movie stars Emilio Estevez, Rob Lowe, Andrew McCarthy, Demi Moore, Judd Nelson, Ally Sheedy, and Mare Winningham as seven friends just out of college?

2) What film is a semi-autobiographical work by director John Boorman about a nine-year-old boy growing up in London during the WWII blitz?

3) Who plays Goldie Hawn's squad leader in *Private Benjamin*?

4) *Pee-Wee's Big Adventure* was the film debut for Pee-Wee Herman; it was also the feature film debut for what director?

5) What movie has a deranged Glenn Close boiling a bunny?

6) What actor says, "Say hello to my little friend!"?

7) In *Trading Places*, what two actors play the Duke brothers whose one dollar bet precipitates the trade in places between Eddie Murphy and Dan Aykroyd?

8) In the *National Lampoon* series of vacation movies, what is the full name of Chevy Chase's character?

9) What film has the tagline "Sleep all day. Party all night. Never grow old. Never die. It's fun to be a vampire"?

10) Who plays Indiana Jones' former girlfriend Marion Ravenwood in *Raiders of the Lost Ark*?

Quiz 16 Answers

1) *St. Elmo's Fire*
2) *Hope and Glory*
3) Eileen Brennan
4) Tim Burton
5) *Fatal Attraction*
6) Al Pacino – *Scarface*
7) Don Ameche and Ralph Bellamy
8) Clark Griswold
9) *The Lost Boys*
10) Karen Allen

Quiz 17

1) "They're here!" is from what horror film?

2) Canada's most famous hosers, Bob and Doug McKenzie, star in *Strange Brew*; what two actors play the McKenzie brothers?

3) Who has the title role in *The Incredible Shrinking Woman*?

4) What Stanly Kubrick film follows Private Joker through boot camp and on to Vietnam?

5) Meryl Streep plays a Holocaust survivor and won her first Best Actress Oscar for what film?

6) What are the names of the brothers played by John Belushi and Dan Aykroyd in *The Blues Brothers*?

7) What comedic character says, "Life moves pretty fast; if you don't stop and look around once in a while, you could miss it"?

8) What western stars Kevin Kline, Danny Glover, Kevin Costner, John Cleese, Jeff Goldblum, and Linda Hunt?

9) In *Nine to Five*, who are the three actresses who play female co-workers

who get revenge on their horrible boss played by Dabney Coleman?

10) Who plays Debbie Thompson, the woman Tom Hanks' character is going to marry, in *Bachelor Party*?

Quiz 17 Answers

1) *Poltergeist*
2) Rick Moranis and Dave Thomas
3) Lily Tomlin
4) *Full Metal Jacket*
5) *Sophie's Choice*
6) Jake and Elwood Blues
7) Ferris Bueller – played by Matthew Broderick in *Ferris Bueller's Day Off*
8) *Silverado*
9) Jane Fonda, Lily Tomlin, Dolly Parton
10) Tawny Kitaen

Quiz 18

1) Who provides the voice for sultry Jessica Rabbit in *Who Framed Roger Rabbit*?
2) Who won a Best Supporting Actor Oscar for *The Untouchables*?
3) What is the name of Kurt Russell's character in *Escape from New York*?
4) What comedy that spawned two sequels is set in 1954 and has a group of Florida high school students trying to lose their virginity?
5) The Australian film *Breaker Morant* starring Edward Woodward is set during what war?
6) What singer plays the Goblin King in *Labyrinth*?
7) What is the name of the town where *Bill and Ted's Excellent Adventure* is set?
8) Who won a Best Actor Oscar for *Gandhi*?
9) What are the last names of the two reluctant detectives played by Judge Reinhold and John Ashton who help Eddie Murphy in *Beverly Hills Cop*?
10) Who was the inspiration for the character of Biff Tannen, the bully in *Back to the Future*?

Quiz 18 Answers

1) Kathleen Turner
2) Sean Connery
3) Snake Plissken

4) *Porky's*
5) Boer War – 1899 to 1902 between the British Empire and the two Boer states, the South African Republic and the Orange Free State
6) David Bowie
7) San Dimas
8) Ben Kingsley
9) Rosewood and Taggart
10) Donald Trump

Quiz 19

1) What biographical film directed by Sydney Pollack and starring Robert Redford and Meryl Streep won nine Oscars?
2) Where is the resort where Baby and Johnny fall in love in *Dirty Dancing*?
3) What movie is based on a Pulitzer Prize winning play and won the Best Picture Oscar and has the tagline "The funny, touching and totally irresistible story of a working relationship that became a 25-year friendship"?
4) What crime thriller was the Coen brothers' first movie?
5) What movie is based on the true story of the all black 54th Massachusetts Volunteer Infantry regiment during the American Civil War?
6) What Mel Gibson and Sissy Spacek film is about a man and his family fighting the bank and severe storms to hold on to their farm?
7) What film produced the first Best Actress Oscar nomination for a science fiction film?
8) What is the name of the fictional office building that is the setting for *Die Hard*?
9) What character did Michael J. Fox play in *Back to the Future*?
10) What is the first name of Dustin Hoffman's female character in *Tootsie*?

Quiz 19 Answers

1) *Out of Africa*
2) Catskill Mountains in New York
3) *Driving Miss Daisy*
4) *Blood Simple*
5) *Glory*
6) *The River*
7) *Aliens* – Sigourney Weaver
8) Nakatomi Plaza

9) Marty McFly
10) Dorothy

Quiz 20

1) What actress says the line "No wire hangers, ever!"?
2) What Michael J. Fox film has the tagline "He always wanted to be special... but he never expected this!"?
3) During filming of *The Blues Brothers*, they had a special budget for what during night shoots?
4) *Ladyhawke* features two cursed lovers; Michelle Pfeiffer spends her days in the form of a hawk and Rutger Hauer spends his nights as a what?
5) Nicolas Cage and Holly Hunter play a childless couple who steal a baby in *Raising Arizona*; who directed the film?
6) What two actors play Lewis and Gilbert, the lead nerds, in *Revenge of the Nerds*?
7) What movie has the tagline "The only winning move is not to play"?
8) What character says, "Greed, for lack of a better word, is good"?
9) What was Kathleen Turner's first feature film?
10) Who directed *Ferris Bueller's Day Off*, *Uncle Buck*, *Weird Science*, and *Planes, Trains and Automobiles*?

Quiz 20 Answers

1) Faye Dunaway – *Mommie Dearest*
2) *Teen Wolf*
3) Cocaine
4) Wolf
5) Joel and Ethan Coen
6) Robert Carradine and Anthony Edwards
7) *War Games*
8) Gordon Gekko – played by Michael Douglas in *Wall Street*
9) *Body Heat*
10) John Hughes

Quiz 21

1) Who plays the title role in *The Princess Bride*?
2) In *Back to the Future*, how fast does the DeLorean have to go to time travel?

3) Who plays the title role in *Robocop*?

4) Who plays Elliot Ness in *The Untouchables*?

5) Who directed *Blade Runner*?

6) In *Splash*, what business is Tom Hanks' character in?

7) In *Planes, Trains, and Automobiles*, John Candy's character Del Griffith sells what for a living?

8) What is Bill Murray's character name in *Caddyshack*?

9) In *Biloxi Blues* starring Matthew Broderick, a group of young recruits is going through boot camp during WWII in Biloxi, Mississippi; who plays the sadistic drill sergeant?

10) What film stars Richard Gere as a young man at a Navy Officer Candidate School and won Louis Gossett Jr. a Best Supporting Actor Oscar?

Quiz 21 Answers

1) Robin Wright

2) 88 mph

3) Peter Weller

4) Kevin Costner

5) Ridley Scott

6) Produce – It was a family fruits and vegetables business.

7) Shower curtain rings

8) Carl Spackler

9) Christopher Walken

10) *An Officer and a Gentleman*

Quiz 22

1) In the James Bond film *Octopussy* with Roger Moore, who plays the title role?

2) What is the name of the character from the future George Carlin plays in *Bill and Ted's Excellent Adventure*?

3) What classic play is *Roxanne* based on?

4) Who plays the nerdy florist in *Little Shop of Horrors*?

5) Who directed *Sixteen Candles*?

6) What was Monty Python's last movie?

7) In *Goonies*, what it the name of the pirate whose treasure they are searching for?

8) In *3 Men and a Baby*, three bachelors must take care of a baby; what

actors play the three bachelors?

9) What actor won his first Oscar for *Arthur* at the age of 77?

10) An American corporate executive is sent to Scotland to purchase an entire fishing village for an oil company and finds himself charmed by the people and culture; what is the film?

Quiz 22 Answers

1) Maud Adams
2) Rufus
3) *Cyrano de Bergerac*
4) Rick Moranis
5) John Hughes
6) *The Meaning of Life*
7) One Eyed Willy
8) Tom Selleck, Ted Danson, Steve Guttenberg
9) Sir John Gielgud
10) *Local Hero* – starring Peter Riegert

Quiz 23

1) What David Lynch film stars Isabella Rossellini, Kyle MacLachlan, Dennis Hopper, Laura Dern, and Dean Stockwell?

2) What boxer's life is depicted in *Raging Bull*?

3) What Ron Howard film starring Steve Martin and Mary Steenburgen centers on the midwestern Buckman family dealing with life; what is the movie?

4) What is the day job of Jennifer Beale's character in *Flashdance*?

5) What film is based on the autobiography of Ron Kovic, an American veteran who was paralyzed during his tour of duty in Vietnam and won Oliver Stone his second Best Director Oscar?

6) Who plays Freddy Krueger in the *Nightmare on Elm Street* films?

7) What is the name of Kevin Costner's character in *Field of Dreams*?

8) In the original script for *Back to the Future*, the time machine wasn't a DeLorean; what was it?

9) In *War Games*, the NORAD supercomputer that almost causes World War III is called what?

10) In *National Lampoon's Vacation*, what is the ultimate destination?

Quiz 23 Answers

1) *Blue Velvet*
2) Jake LaMotta
3) *Parenthood*
4) Welder
5) *Born on the Fourth of July*
6) Robert Englund
7) Ray Kinsella
8) Refrigerator
9) WOPR – for War Operation Plan Response
10) Walley World

Quiz 24

1) What movie features the line "*Carpe diem.* Seize the day, boys. Make your lives extraordinary"?
2) What movie won Sissy Spacek the Best Actress Oscar?
3) In what Werner Herzog film does Brian Sweeney Fitzgerald try to build an opera house in the jungle?
4) For what film did Dustin Hoffman win his second Best Actor Oscar?
5) In *Blind Date*, who plays Bruce Willis' blind date?
6) What film has Tom Hanks and Shelley Long struggling to repair a hopelessly dilapidated house?
7) What Woody Allen film features Mia Farrow, Barbara Hershey, Carrie Fisher, Michael Caine, Dianne Wiest, Maureen O'Sullivan, Max von Sydow, J.T. Walsh, John Turturro, Daniel Stern, Julie Kavner, Lewis Black, and Julia Louis-Dreyfus?
8) What was the number one U.S. box office film released in the 1980s?
9) In *The Woman in Red*, Gene Wilder plays a man who desperately tries to cheat on his wife with a woman he saw in a red dress; who plays the title role?
10) In *Educating Rita*, 27-year-old hairdresser Rita goes back to finish her education and is assisted by a middle-aged professor played by Michael Caine; who plays the title role?

Quiz 24 Answers

1) *Dead Poets Society* – Robin Williams
2) *Coal Miner's Daughter*
3) *Fitzcarraldo*

4) *Rain Man*
5) Kim Bassinger
6) *The Money Pit*
7) *Hannah and Her Sisters*
8) *E.T.: The Extra-Terrestrial* – 1982
9) Kelly LeBrock
10) Julie Walters

1990s

Quiz 1

1) What Guy Ritchie crime comedy set in London features four friends who find themselves heavily in debt to a local gangster after a crooked card game and hatch a plan to steal the money they need, and things go awry?

2) Who provides the voice for the mouse who is the title character in *Stuart Little*?

3) The creator of *Beavis and Butthead* directed the work comedy *Office Space*; who is he?

4) What film stars Nicole Kidman as a local television weather reporter who wants to be a news anchor and persuades a high school boy to kill her husband who is standing in her way?

5) What film stars Mel Gibson as a wealthy father who refuses to pay the ransom for his kidnapped son and instead offers the money as a reward for the capture of the kidnappers?

6) In *True Lies*, who plays Arnold Schwarzenegger's wife who doesn't know he is a spy?

7) What British comedy has six unemployed steel workers forming a striptease act?

8) What comedy has the tagline "She makes dinner. She does windows. She reads bedtime stories. She's a blessing... in disguise"?

9) Who plays the two crooks in *Home Alone*?

10) What Wesley Snipes film has the tagline "The power of an immortal. The soul of a human. The heart of a hero"?

Quiz 1 Answers

1) *Lock, Stock and Two Smoking Barrels*
2) Michael J. Fox
3) Mike Judge
4) *To Die For*
5) *Ransom*
6) Jamie Lee Curtis
7) *The Full Monty*
8) *Mrs. Doubtfire*
9) Daniel Stern and Joe Pesci

10) *Blade*

Quiz 2

1) In *Tremors*, what actor and actress play the survivalist couple who help battle the giant wormlike creatures?

2) *Seven Years in Tibet* is the true story of mountain climber Heinrich Harrer and his friendship with the young Dalai Lama; who plays Heinrich Harrer?

3) What movie features Judi Dench as Queen Victoria in a story about how she finds solace in her trusted servant Mr. Brown after her husband dies?

4) Jessica Tandy plays elderly Ninny Threadgoode who tells stories about people she used to know in what movie?

5) In *Amistad*, who plays former president John Quincy Adams who makes a plea for the release of the slaves before the U.S. Supreme Court?

6) What movie is the story of reformed Neo Nazi Derek Vinyard and his attempts to keep his brother from going down the same path?

7) What character said, "I just put one foot in front of the other. When I get tired, I sleep. When I get hungry, I eat. When I have to go to the bathroom, I go"?

8) What comedy has the tagline "The fastest hands in the East versus the biggest mouth in the West"?

9) What Merchant and Ivory production features Anthony Hopkins and Emma Thompson as a butler and housekeeper in pre-WWII Britain?

10) What was the first movie based on a John Grisham novel?

Quiz 2 Answers

1) Michael Gross and Reba McEntire
2) Brad Pitt
3) *Mrs Brown*
4) *Fried Green Tomatoes*
5) Anthony Hopkins
6) *American History X*
7) Forrest Gump
8) *Rush Hour*
9) *The Remains of the Day*
10) *The Firm*

Quiz 3

1) What military film has the tagline "In the heart of the nation's capital, in a courthouse of the U.S. government, one man will stop at nothing to keep his honor, and one will stop at nothing to find the truth"?
2) The frenetically paced *Run Lola Run* features three different versions of the same set of events; what country produced the film?
3) Gene Hackman received an Oscar for his portrayal of the sheriff of Big Whiskey in what movie?
4) What is the name of Frances McDormand's character in *Fargo*?
5) In *Pleasantville*, who plays the TV repairmen who sends the siblings back in time?
6) In *The Devil's Advocate*, Keanu Reeves is a lawyer who discovers his boss is Satan; who plays the Devil?
7) Who plays the head of NASA in *Armageddon*?
8) Who plays the title role in *Patch Adams*?
9) In *Notting Hill*, Hugh Grant's character owns and works in a very specialized shop, what kind of shop is it?
10) What crime drama stars Russell Crowe, Guy Pearce, Kevin Spacey, James Cromwell, Danny DeVito and won Kim Basinger a Best Supporting Actress Oscar?

Quiz 3 Answers

1) *A Few Good Men*
2) Germany
3) *Unforgiven*
4) Marge Gunderson
5) Don Knotts
6) Al Pacino
7) Billy Bob Thornton
8) Robin Williams
9) Travel book shop
10) *L.A. Confidential*

Quiz 4

1) What character says, "There's no crying in baseball!"?
2) Who won a Best Adapted Screenplay Oscar for *Sense and Sensibility* and was nominated for a Best Actress Oscar for her performance in the film?

3) What was the second movie to pair Richard Gere and Julia Roberts?

4) What Oscar winning actress plays Tom Hanks' mother in *Philadelphia*?

5) What Disney animated feature has the tagline "This time, the princess saves the prince"?

6) What romantic comedy features Rosie O'Donnell, Rita Wilson, and Meg Ryan?

7) *Shine* is based on the true story of Australian pianist David Helfgott who suffered a breakdown and spent many years in an institution before eventually returning to the concert hall; who plays David Helfgott?

8) Who plays the title role in *The Big Lebowski*?

9) Who is the only actor to reprise their role in all three movies made in the 1990s based on Tom Clancy novels featuring the character Jack Ryan?

10) What Tim Burton movie has the tagline "His story will touch you, even though he can't"?

Quiz 4 Answers

1) Jimmy Dugan – played by Tom Hanks in *A League of Their Own*

2) Emma Thompson

3) *Runaway Bride*

4) Joanne Woodward

5) *Mulan*

6) *Sleepless in Seattle*

7) Geoffrey Rush – He won the Best Actor Oscar.

8) David Huddleston – The Dude or Jeff Lebowski played by Jeff Bridges is mistaken for The Big Lebowski character.

9) James Earl Jones – appeared as Admiral James Greer in *The Hunt for Red October* (1990), *Patriot Games* (1992), *Clear and Present Danger* (1994)

10) *Edward Scissorhands*

Quiz 5

1) What Quentin Tarantino movie is about two mob hitmen, a boxer, a gangster's wife, and a pair of diner bandits?

2) Who is the arch enemy of Austin Powers?

3) In *Awakenings* starring Robin Williams and Robert De Niro; what is the experimental drug that the patients are given to bring them out of their catatonic state?

4) What actress says, "You had me at hello"?

5) Who two actors play Fred Flintstone and Barney Rubble in *The Flintstones*?

6) What movie has Tobie Maguire and Reese Witherspoon zapped back to the 1950s?

7) What film was Kevin Costner's directorial debut?

8) Bruce Willis plays a time traveler in what movie?

9) Nicolas Cage won a Best Actor Oscar for his portrayal of an alcoholic screenwriter who has lost everything in what film?

10) *Doctor Dolittle* is based on the stories of what author?

Quiz 5 Answers

1) *Pulp Fiction*
2) Dr. Evil
3) L–Dopa
4) Renee Zellweger – *Jerry Maguire*
5) John Goodman and Rick Moranis
6) *Pleasantville*
7) *Dances with Wolves*
8) *12 Monkeys*
9) *Leaving Las Vegas*
10) Hugh Lofting

Quiz 6

1) Who plays Jack Ryan in *The Hunt for Red October*?

2) What Oscar winning crime thriller has the tagline "To enter the mind of a killer she must challenge the mind of a madman"?

3) In *Coneheads*, what planet are the Coneheads from?

4) For what film did Tom Hanks win his first Best Actor Oscar?

5) What comedy has the tagline "He's up past his bedtime in the city that never sleeps"?

6) Who provides the voice of Jane in Disney's animated *Tarzan*?

7) What film character's traditional greeting is "Good morning! And in case I don't see you, good afternoon, good evening, and good night"?

8) Susan Sarandon won a Best Actress Oscar for her portrayal of a nun who befriends a convicted killer on death row in what movie?

9) What character says, "You can't handle the truth!"?

10) In *The Truman Show*, what is the title character's last name?

Quiz 6 Answers

1) Alec Baldwin
2) *The Silence of the Lambs*
3) Remulak
4) *Philadelphia*
5) *Home Alone 2: Lost in New York*
6) Minnie Driver
7) Truman – played by Jim Carrey in *The Truman Show*
8) *Dead Man Walking*
9) Colonel Nathan Jessep – played by Jack Nicholson in *A Few Good Men*
10) Burbank

Quiz 7

1) In *Groundhog Day*, each repeating day starts with what song on the radio?
2) What was the first James Bond film where M, the head of MI6, is played by a woman?
3) What movie has the tagline "The monster movie that breaks new ground"?
4) In *Sleepless in Seattle*, Sam's sister gets emotional describing the plot to *An Affair to Remember*; Sam and his brother-in-law poke fun at her by getting emotional describing what less romantic film?
5) For what mob story did Joe Pesci win a Best Supporting Actor Oscar?
6) What Kevin Costner film has the tagline "For the good of all men, and the love of one woman, he fought to uphold justice by breaking the law"?
7) In *Election*, Reese Witherspoon plays Tracy Flick, an obsessive high school overachiever who is determined to be student body president; who plays the teacher who interferes in her plans and suffers the consequences?
8) What animated Disney movie follows an ant on a mission to save his colony from grasshoppers?
9) What three films did Tom Cruise and Nicole Kidman star together in during the 1990s?
10) *The Shawshank Redemption* is based on a short story by Stephen King. For the movie, they dropped the first part of the story title which is a major Hollywood star's name; what is the name?

Quiz 7 Answers

1) Sonny and Cher's "I Got You Babe"
2) *GoldenEye* – Judi Dench
3) *Tremors*
4) *The Dirty Dozen*
5) *Goodfellas*
6) *Robin Hood: Prince of Thieves*
7) Matthew Broderick
8) *A Bug's Life*
9) *Days of Thunder* (1990), *Far and Away* (1992), *Eyes Wide Shut* (1999)
10) Rita Hayworth – The Stephen King short story title is *Rita Hayworth and the Shawshank Redemption.* Rita Hayworth is the first poster Andy has on the wall in his cell; the prisoners are also watching the Rita Hayworth film *Gilda* in one scene.

Quiz 8

1) What Best Picture Oscar winner has the tagline "Whoever saves one life saves the world entire"?
2) Who plays the park creator John Hammond in *Jurassic Park?*
3) In *Terminator* 2, who plays the T-1000 Terminator sent to kill John Connor?
4) Who plays the character whose dismembered body is fed into the woodchipper in *Fargo?*
5) What is the name of Kevin Spacey's character in *The Usual Suspects?*
6) What comedy has the tagline "Protecting the earth from the scum of the universe"?
7) What book does Forrest Gump keep in his suitcase?
8) What historical character did Mel Gibson play in *Braveheart?*
9) What comedy has the tagline "Love is in the hair"?
10) *Quiz Show* is based on a true 1950s game show cheating scandal; Ralph Fiennes plays what real person who was a member of one of America's leading literary families and became a national celebrity based on his fraudulent wins?

Quiz 8 Answers

1) *Schindler's List*
2) Richard Attenborough
3) Robert Patrick

4) Steve Buscemi
5) Keyser Soze or Roger "Verbal" Kint
6) *Men in Black*
7) *Curious George*
8) William Wallace
9) *There's Something About Mary*
10) Charles Van Doren

Quiz 9

1) What was the first animated film to gross $200 million in the U.S.?
2) Who sings the title song in *Pretty Woman*?
3) Who wrote the novel on which *Jurassic Park* is based?
4) *The People vs. Larry Flynt* is about the controversial pornography publisher and how he became a defender of free speech; who plays Larry Flynt?
5) After a prank goes wrong, four boys are sent to a reformatory where they are physically and sexually abused; many years later they get their chance at revenge; what is the movie?
6) What film features Jim, Oz, Finch and Kevin as four friends who make a pact to lose their virginity by prom night?
7) What comedy has the tagline "I'm Back, Baby!"?
8) *Fear and Loathing in Las Vegas* is based on what author's book about his psychedelic road trip across western America?
9) What was the most expensive Hollywood film made in the 1990s?
10) In *Matrix*, what is the name of the legendary hacker played by Laurence Fishburne who awakens Neo to the real world?

Quiz 9 Answers

1) *Aladdin*
2) Roy Orbison – He co-wrote and recorded the song "Pretty Woman" in 1964; its use in the movie revitalized interest in his music although he had died in 1988.
3) Michael Crichton
4) Woody Harrelson
5) *Sleepers* – starring Kevin Bacon, Brad Pitt, Jason Patric, Minnie Driver, Dustin Hoffman, Robert De Niro
6) *American Pie*
7) *Austin Powers: The Spy Who Shagged Me*
8) Hunter S. Thompson

9) *Titanic* - $200 million
10) Morpheus

Quiz 10

1) In *Mission Impossible*, who plays Jim Phelps?
2) In *Four Weddings and a Funeral*, who plays the American Carrie that Hugh Grant's character falls in love with?
3) What romantic comedy has the tagline "Someone you pass on the street may already be the love of your life"?
4) Who provides the voice for Captain John Smith in Disney's *Pocahontas*?
5) In *Ace Ventura: Pet Detective*, Ace is hired to find a football team's mascot; what kind of animal is it?
6) What film based on an E.M. Forster novel and directed by James Ivory stars Vanessa Redgrave, Anthony Hopkins, Emma Thompson, and Helena Bonham Carter?
7) In *The Fisher King*, Robin Williams plays a deranged homeless man who is looking for what artifact?
8) What Ralph Fiennes and Juliette Binoche period piece won nine Oscars?
9) What western has about 25% of its dialogue in a language other than English?
10) What is the name of the terrorist organization the fight clubs evolve into in *Fight Club*?

Quiz 10 Answers

1) Jon Voight
2) Andie MacDowell
3) *You've Got Mail*
4) Mel Gibson
5) Dolphin
6) *Howards End*
7) Holy Grail
8) *The English Patient*
9) *Dances with Wolves* – The Lakota language is used heavily.
10) Project Mayhem

Quiz 11

1) What romantic comedy has the tagline "What if someone you never met, someone you never saw, someone you never knew was the only

someone for you?"

2) What film is about a group of friends growing up in the Los Angeles ghetto during the 1980s and was John Singleton's directorial debut?

3) In what year is *Apollo 13* set?

4) What crime thriller stars Michael Douglas as an unemployed defense worker frustrated with life and becoming increasingly violent until he ends up being shot down by a policeman played by Robert Duvall?

5) In *The Santa Clause*, what is Tim Allen's character name?

6) What movie stars Michelle Pfeiffer as a former Marine turned teacher who struggles to connect with her students in an inner-city school?

7) In what film does a disturbed romance novel fan gush, "I am your number one fan"?

8) What animated film was the number one grossing movie worldwide in 1994?

9) In *Demolition Man*, Sylvester Stallone plays John Spartan who is revived from suspended animation into a very different future world. In one scene, he visits a restroom and finds there is no toilet paper; he discovers that toilet paper has been replaced by what?

10) In what movie does Bruce Willis play Korben Dallas?

Quiz 11 Answers

1) *Sleepless in Seattle*

2) *Boyz n the Hood*

3) 1970

4) *Falling Down*

5) Scott Calvin

6) *Dangerous Minds*

7) *Misery*

8) *The Lion King*

9) Three seashells – It is never explained how the three seashells are used in place of toilet paper.

10) *The Fifth Element*

Quiz 12

1) What comedy has the tagline "He's having the worst day of his life... over, and over..."?

2) What crime thriller has the tagline "Let he who is without sin try to survive"?

3) What historical movie has the tagline "His passion captivated a

woman. His courage inspired a nation. His heart defied a king"?

4) Who plays Louise in *Thelma & Louise*?

5) During what war is *The Last of the Mohicans* set?

6) The 1978 French film *La Cage aux Folles* was remade as what American film?

7) What movie is a remake of 1940's *The Shop Around the Corner* starring James Stewart and Margaret Sullavan?

8) In *Dances with Wolves*, who plays Stands With A Fist, a white woman who was raised by the Sioux?

9) What film based on a David Mamet play and set in a real estate office stars Al Pacino, Kevin Spacey, Jack Lemmon, Ed Harris, Alan Arkin, Alec Baldwin, and Jonathan Pryce?

10) Who plays the judge in *My Cousin Vinny*?

Quiz 12 Answers

1) *Groundhog Day*

2) *Se7en*

3) *Braveheart*

4) Susan Sarandon

5) French and Indian War – 1754 to 1763

6) *The Birdcage*

7) *You've Got Mail* – In the original, they were employees at a leather goods store and unknowingly fall in love through the mail as anonymous pen pals.

8) Mary McDonnell

9) *Glengarry Glen Ross*

10) Fred Gwynne – his final feature film

Quiz 13

1) What adventure fantasy has the tagline "It's a jungle in there!"?

2) In *I Know What You Did Last Summer*, four teens hit and apparently kill a pedestrian in a car accident; the teens are played by Sarah Michelle Gellar, Jennifer Love Hewitt, Ryan Phillippe, and who?

3) What movie features Karl Childers, a simple man hospitalized since childhood for murder, who is released to start a new life in a small town?

4) In *A Nightmare Before Christmas*, what is the name of the Pumpkin King of Halloween Town who tries to take over Christmas?

5) What film based on a John Grisham novel stars Sandra Bullock, Samuel

L. Jackson, Kiefer Sutherland and Matthew McConaughey?

6) What is the name of Tim Burton's biopic about a low budget film director of the 1950s and 1960s?

7) Who won a Best Original Screenplay Oscar for *Good Will Hunting*?

8) *Malcolm X* is based on the 1965 book *The Autobiography of Malcom X* written by what author in collaboration with Malcolm X?

9) What thriller has the tagline "Paul Sheldon used to write for a living. Now, he's writing to stay alive"?

10) Who plays the title roles in *Dumb and Dumber*?

Quiz 13 Answers

1) *Jumanji*
2) Freddie Prinze Jr.
3) *Sling Blade*
4) Jack Skellington
5) *A Time to Kill*
6) *Ed Wood*
7) Matt Damon and Ben Affleck
8) Alex Haley
9) *Misery*
10) Jim Carrey and Jeff Daniels

Quiz 14

1) What film starring Ian McKellen and Brendan Fraser focuses on the last days of *Frankenstein* director James Whale?

2) In *Basic Instinct*, Michael Douglas plays a detective investigating a brutal murder, and Sharon Stone's character is a suspect. What is the murder weapon?

3) What was the last feature film of Sir John Gielgud in which he plays the Pope?

4) Who plays the title role in Oliver Stone's *Nixon*?

5) What is the title of the first sequel to *Jurassic Park*?

6) Who plays the title role in the French film *Cyrano de Bergerac*?

7) Who plays Obi-Wan Kenobi in *Star Wars: Episode I – The Phantom Menace*?

8) What movie stars Geena Davis as a suburban homemaker who begins to remember parts of her previous life as a lethal secret agent and must fight to save her life?

9) What romantic comedy has the tagline "She walked off the street, into

his life and stole his heart"?

10) What actor says, "I see dead people"?

Quiz 14 Answers

1) *Gods and Monsters*
2) Ice pick
3) *Elizabeth* – 1998
4) Anthony Hopkins
5) *The Lost World: Jurassic Park*
6) Gerard Depardieu
7) Ewan McGregor
8) *The Long Kiss Goodnight*
9) *Pretty Woman*
10) Haley Joel Osment – *The Sixth Sense*

Quiz 15

1) In *The Last of the Mohicans*, who plays the central character Hawkeye who is a white man adopted by the Mohicans?
2) What film features Al Pacino as a policeman hunting down a crew of bank robbers led by Robert De Niro?
3) What Jim Carrey comedy has him inserting himself into the life of Matthew Broderick?
4) Who is the voice of the beast in Disney's animated *Beauty and the Beast*?
5) In *The Mummy*, who plays English librarian Evelyn Carnahan?
6) Robin Williams won a Best Supporting Actor Oscar for what film?
7) What slasher film has the tagline "Someone has taken their love of scary movies one step too far. Solving this mystery is going to be murder"?
8) Who directed *Casino* marking the eighth time the director and Robert De Niro had worked together?
9) Who plays Bobby Boucher's football coach in *The Waterboy*?
10) What movie has the tagline "The greatest trick the devil ever pulled was to convince the world he didn't exist"?

Quiz 15 Answers

1) Daniel Day-Lewis
2) *Heat*
3) *The Cable Guy*

4) Robby Benson
5) Rachel Weisz
6) *Good Will Hunting*
7) *Scream*
8) Martin Scorsese – The eight films up to that point were *Mean Streets* (1973), *Taxi Driver* (1976), *New York, New York* (1977), *Raging Bull* (1980), *The King of Comedy* (1983), *Goodfellas* (1990), *Cape Fear* (1991), *Casino* (1995).
9) Henry Winkler
10) *The Usual Suspects*

Quiz 16

1) In *Independence Day*, what is used to defeat the aliens?
2) What movie stars Kevin Spacey as a middle-aged suburban father who becomes infatuated with his daughter's best friend?
3) In *Copycat*, Sigourney Weaver plays a psychologist who specializes in serial killers; who plays Daryll Lee Cullum, the serial killer who tried to kill her?
4) What Nicolas Cage film has the tagline "They were deadly on the ground. Now they have wings"?
5) What was Pixar's first feature film?
6) In *City Slickers*, three middle-aged friends go on an adventure holiday driving cattle; who won a Best Supporting Actor Oscar for their role as the trail boss Curly?
7) What film set primarily in New Zealand won a Best Supporting Actress Oscar for Anna Paquin and a Best Actress Oscar for Holly Hunter?
8) Who plays the U.S. Vice President in *Air Force One*?
9) What romantic comedy has the tagline "Michael and Julianne have been best friends for years - but they were never more than that - until he popped the question - to someone else"?
10) Billy Bob Thornton won a Best Adapted Screenplay Oscar for what film?

Quiz 16 Answers

1) Computer virus – The idea was taken from H.G. Wells' *The War of the Worlds* where the Martians are killed by bacteria and viruses.
2) *American Beauty*
3) Harry Connick Jr.
4) *Con Air*
5) *Toy Story*

6) Jack Palance
7) *The Piano*
8) Glenn Close
9) *My Best Friend's Wedding* – starring Julia Roberts and Dermot Mulroney
10) *Sling Blade*

Quiz 17

1) What film starring Jason Schwartzman and Bill Murray is about a 15-year-old boy who is king of extracurricular activities at his private preparatory school and gets involved in an odd love triangle?
2) Whoopi Goldberg won a Best Supporting Actress Oscar for what film?
3) Who plays the title role in *Elizabeth* detailing the early reign of Queen Elizabeth I?
4) What was the first feature film with Tom Hanks and Meg Ryan?
5) What is the name of Jeff Bridge's character in *The Big Lebowski*?
6) What Coen brothers film centers on Prohibition era gangsters?
7) What Michael Douglas movie has the tagline "What do you get for the man who has everything?"
8) What is the name of Whoopi Goldberg's psychic character in *Ghost*?
9) What two westerns won Best Picture Oscars in the 1990s?
10) Kevin Smith's *Clerks* is loosely based on what classic piece of 14th century literature?

Quiz 17 Answers

1) *Rushmore*
2) *Ghost*
3) Cate Blanchett
4) *Joe Versus the Volcano*
5) The Dude or Jeff Lebowski
6) *Miller's Crossing*
7) *The Game*
8) Oda Mae Brown
9) *Dances with Wolves* and *Unforgiven*
10) *The Divine Comedy* by Dante – The main protagonist, Dante Hicks, gets his name from this, and there are nine breaks in the film to represent the nine rings of hell.

Quiz 18

1) Who plays the female internal affairs detective Martin Riggs falls for in *Lethal Weapon 3*?
2) What are the names of the four turtles in *Teenage Mutant Ninja Turtles*?
3) In *Edward Scissorhands*, who plays the inventor who creates Edward?
4) Who plays U.S. President Beck in *Deep Impact* about the efforts to prevent a comet from destroying the Earth?
5) What was the number one U.S. box office film released in the 1990s?
6) What early Quentin Tarantino film has the tagline "Seven total strangers team up for the perfect crime. They don't know each other's name. But they've got each other's color"?
7) What well known actor made his film debut in *Critters 3*?
8) What movie features a researcher who comes under personal and professional attack when he decides to appear in a *60 Minutes* expose on Big Tobacco?
9) Cameron Diaz's film debut was in what comedy with Jim Carrey?
10) What Quentin Tarantino film stars Pam Grier, Samuel L. Jackson, Robert Forster, Bridget Fonda, Michael Keaton, and Robert De Niro?

Quiz 18 Answers

1) Rene Russo
2) Raphael, Leonardo, Donatello, Michelangelo
3) Vincent Price
4) Morgan Freeman
5) *Titanic* – 1997
6) *Reservoir Dogs*
7) Leonardo DiCaprio
8) *The Insider*
9) *The Mask*
10) *Jackie Brown*

Quiz 19

1) What Robert Altman film stars Tim Robbins as a Hollywood studio executive who is receiving death threats and murders a writer he believes is responsible?
2) Who wrote and directed *The Sixth Sense*?
3) Who is the writer and director for both *Sleepless in Seattle* and *You've Got Mail*?

4) In *Sister Act*, what is the stage name of Whoopi Goldberg's character?
5) In *Thunderheart*, who plays the FBI agent with Sioux background who is sent to a reservation to investigate a murder and has to come to terms with his heritage?
6) In *Fight Club*, who plays the nameless first-person narrator?
7) In *Dogma*, two renegade angels played by Matt Damon and Ben Affleck try to exploit a loophole to re-enter heaven; who plays the role of God?
8) In *The Cider House Rules*, Tobey Maguire plays an orphan who is trained to be a doctor by Dr. Larch, the orphanage director; who won a Best Supporting Actor Oscar for his portrayal of Dr. Larch?
9) In *Ghost*, what does Sam always say instead of saying "I love you"?
10) What film has a mobster named Chili Palmer who goes to Hollywood and gets involved in the movie business?

Quiz 19 Answers

1) *The Player*
2) M. Night Shyamalan
3) Nora Ephron
4) Deloris Van Cartier
5) Val Kilmer
6) Edward Norton
7) Alanis Morissette
8) Michael Caine
9) Ditto
10) *Get Shorty* – starring John Travolta

Quiz 20

1) What Matt Damon film explores the world of high stakes poker?
2) At 24 minutes and 52 seconds of screen time, this Best Actor Oscar winning performance is the second shortest ever, and the movie also won the Best Picture Oscar. Who is the actor?
3) Who won an acting Oscar for *My Cousin Vinny*?
4) What movie has Arnold Schwarzenegger as a U.S. Marshal protecting Vanessa Williams?
5) Whose poster is on the wall concealing the tunnel when Andy Dufresne escapes in *The Shawshank Redemption*?
6) In *Days of Thunder*, who plays Cole Trickle's crew chief Harry Hogge?
7) In *The Rock*, who plays General Hummel who threatens to attack San Francisco with nerve gas?

8) Who plays the part of Cruella de Vil in *101 Dalmatians*?

9) What was the first Hollywood film released on DVD?

10) Based on the Anne Rice novel, *Interview with the Vampire: The Vampire Chronicles* tells the story of Louis who was turned into a vampire by Lestat; who plays Louis?

Quiz 20 Answers

1) *Rounders*
2) Anthony Hopkins – *The Silence of the Lambs*
3) Marisa Tomei – best supporting actress
4) *Eraser*
5) Raquel Welch – *One Million Years B.C.* movie poster
6) Robert Duvall
7) Ed Harris
8) Glenn Close
9) *Twister* – 1997
10) Brad Pitt

Quiz 21

1) What war film has the tagline "There was only one man left in the family, and the mission was to save him"?

2) What was Pixar's first sequel film?

3) What film takes place primarily at Cold Mountain Penitentiary?

4) Who plays Dr. Niko Tatopolous who battles to stop the monster in *Godzilla*?

5) Who does Babe the pig work for?

6) In *Speed*, what speed does the bus have to maintain to avoid exploding?

7) Who plays Catwoman in *Batman Returns*?

8) What independent film had a $60,000 budget and grossed almost $250 million worldwide?

9) What character is the heroine of *The Silence of the Lambs*?

10) Michael Clarke Duncan plays a death row inmate who can work miracles in *The Green Mile*; what is the name of his character?

Quiz 21 Answers

1) *Saving Private Ryan*
2) *Toy Story 2*
3) *The Green Mile*

4) Matthew Broderick
5) Farmer Hoggett
6) 50 mph
7) Michelle Pfeiffer
8) *The Blair Witch Project*
9) Clarice Starling
10) John Coffey

Quiz 22

1) In *Sleepy Hollow*, Johnny Depp plays Ichabod Crane; who plays the headless horseman?
2) What was the last film Stanley Kubrick directed starring Tom Cruise and Nicole Kidman as a married couple who explore their sexual fantasies?
3) Who plays the Riddler in *Batman Forever*?
4) Johnny Depp plays an undercover FBI agent who infiltrates the mafia and begins identifying with the mob life in what film?
5) What Ridley Scott film about two female best friends is one of the very few films ever to produce two Best Actress Oscar nominations?
6) What Christopher Guest comedy is about an amateur musical production to celebrate the 150th anniversary of a small Missouri town?
7) For what romance comedy did Jack Nicholson win his second Best Actor Oscar?
8) What film stars Stanley Tucci and Tony Shalhoub as Italian immigrant brothers who attempt to save their restaurant by holding a special feast?
9) What film stars Jean Reno as an assassin and Natalie Portman in her film debut as a 12-year-old who becomes his protege, so she can avenge her little brother's murder?
10) For what movie did Tommy Lee Jones win a Best Supporting Actor Oscar?

Quiz 22 Answers

1) Christopher Walken
2) *Eyes Wide Shut*
3) Jim Carrey
4) *Donnie Brasco*
5) *Thelma & Louise*
6) *Waiting for Guffman*

7) *As Good as It Gets*
8) *Big Night*
9) *Leon: The Professional*
10) *The Fugitive*

2000s

Quiz 1

1) In *Indiana Jones and the Kingdom of the Crystal Skull*, what young actor teams up with Indiana Jones in the role of Mutt Williams?

2) In *Zoolander*, clueless fashion model Derek Zoolander is brainwashed to kill the prime minister of what country?

3) Jack Nicholson plays a man who has led a safe, predictable life working in the insurance industry; after retiring, he embarks on an unpredictable RV journey to attend his daughter's wedding. What is the movie?

4) What was the top grossing animated film of the 2000s in the U.S.?

5) In *Up*, what is the South American destination that Carl wants to travel to in his house lifted by balloons?

6) "The only one missing from Sophie's wedding is the father of the bride...whichever one he is," is the tagline for what musical?

7) In *Fred Claus*, who plays Santa Claus?

8) In *Finding Nemo,* what kind of fish is Dory?

9) Josh Whedon wrote and directed the science fiction film *Serenity* which was based on his failed network television show; what was the name of the show?

10) What is the name Tom Hanks gives to the volleyball he talks to in *Cast Away*?

Quiz 1 Answers

1) Shia LaBeouf
2) Malaysia
3) *About Schmidt*
4) *Shrek 2*
5) Paradise Falls
6) *Mamma Mia*
7) Paul Giamatti
8) Blue Tang
9) *Firefly*
10) Wilson

Quiz 2

1) What movie is based on a Philip K. Dick short story and stars Tom Cruise as the Chief John Anderton of the PreCrime Division?
2) A lion, zebra, giraffe, and what animal find themselves unexpectedly in the wild in *Madagascar*?
3) A Hawaiian girl adopts an unusual pet who is actually an extra-terrestrial fugitive in what Disney animated film?
4) What Matt Damon film has the tagline "He was the perfect weapon until he became the target"?
5) What actor provides the voice of the lion Aslan in *The Chronicles of Narnia: The Lion, the Witch and the Wardrobe*?
6) In *Slumdog Millionaire*, what is the final answer Jamal gives to win the grand prize?
7) Who plays the title role in *Yes Man*?
8) What cult classic stars Bruce Campbell as Elvis Presley and Ossie Davis as John F. Kennedy who are residents of a nursing home and must battle a mummy?
9) In *Night at the Museum*, what is Ben Stiller's character name?
10) *Quills* centers on the exploits of the French author the Marquis de Sade; who plays the Marquis de Sade?

Quiz 2 Answers

1) *Minority Report*
2) Hippo
3) *Lilo & Stitch*
4) *The Bourne Identity*
5) Liam Neeson
6) Aramis – the third musketeer in *The Three Musketeers*
7) Jim Carrey
8) *Bubba Ho-Tep*
9) Larry Daley
10) Geoffrey Rush

Quiz 3

1) Who plays Gandalf in *The Lord of the Rings: The Return of the King*?
2) What is the name of Uma Thurman's assassin character in *Kill Bill: Vol. 1*?
3) In *The Legend of Bagger Vance*, Matt Damon portrays Rannulph Junuh

who plays a match against what two real-life golfers?

4) For what movie did Hilary Swank win her first Best Actress Oscar?

5) In *Love Actually*, who plays the aging rocker Billy Mack?

6) What Martin Scorsese film set in 1863 stars Leonardo DiCaprio, Daniel Day-Lewis, Cameron Diaz, Jim Broadbent, John C. Reilly, Henry Thomas, Liam Neeson, and Brendan Gleeson?

7) In *Welcome to Mooseport*, Ray Romano plays a small-town businessman running for mayor against a former U.S. President played by who?

8) What animated film starring Bill Hader, Anna Faris, James Caan, and Bruce Campbell is based on a popular 1978 children's book by Judi Barrett and Ron Barrett?

9) "They were alone in the middle of nowhere. It's watching. It's waiting. It's hungry." is a tagline for what horror movie whose main characters are a brother and sister?

10) In *Superbad*, Seth and Evan are best friends in the last weeks of high school who spend a long day trying to get enough alcohol for a party they are invited to. What two actors play Seth and Evan?

Quiz 3 Answers

1) Ian McKellen
2) The Bride
3) Bobby Jones and Walter Hagen
4) *Boys Don't Cry*
5) Bill Nighy
6) *Gangs of New York*
7) Gene Hackman
8) *Cloudy with a Chance of Meatballs*
9) *Jeepers Creepers*
10) Jonah Hill and Michael Cera

Quiz 4

1) The Tom Hanks movie *The Terminal* was inspired by a man who lived at the departure lounge of what international airport for 18 years?

2) What movie is the true story of mathematician John Nash?

3) *The Lord of the Rings: The Return of the King* (2003) is tied for the most Oscars ever; what movie had the second most Oscar wins in the 2000s?

4) What film set in Warsaw during WWII won Adrian Brody a Best Actor Oscar?

5) What was the first Pixar film with human protagonists?

6) What soundtrack became just the third film soundtrack ever to win the Album of the Year Grammy?

7) Who plays James T. Kirk in *Star Trek*?

8) In *Anger Management*, who plays Dr. Buddy Rydell who is assigned to treat Adam Sandler's character?

9) Who plays Commodious in *Gladiator*?

10) What film starring Don Cheadle has the tagline "When a country descended into madness and the world turned its back, one man had to make a choice"?

Quiz 4 Answers

1) Charles de Gaulle Airport
2) *A Beautiful Mind* – starring Russell Crowe
3) *Slumdog Millionaire* – eight Oscars
4) *The Pianist*
5) *The Incredibles*
6) *O Brother, Where Art Thou?*
7) Chris Pine
8) Jack Nicholson
9) Joaquin Phoenix
10) *Hotel Rwanda*

Quiz 5

1) What company does Tom Hanks work for in *Cast Away*?

2) What Best Actor Oscar winner provides the voice for Doc Hudson, the town judge and physician, in *Cars*?

3) A woman helps bring some life to a rigidly moralistic community through the creation of her confections; what is the movie?

4) In the animated film *Coraline*, an 11-year-old girl finds a strangely idealized parallel world; who provides the voice for Coraline?

5) In *Cheaper by the Dozen*, what actor and actress play the father and mother to 12 children?

6) For what movie did Julia Roberts win a Best Actress Oscar?

7) Who wrote and stars in *My Big Fat Greek Wedding*?

8) In *Lost in Translation*, a faded movie star forms an unlikely bond with a young woman. What country is the movie set in?

9) What romantic zombie comedy stars Simon Pegg, Nick Frost and Bill Nighy?

10) Reese Witherspoon stars as a rising fashion designer in New York who

2) *Bridget Jones's Diary*
3) Homer's *Odyssey*
4) Thermopylae
5) *Remember the Titans*
6) George Clooney – plays Danny Ocean
7) Cullen
8) *Mystic River*
9) *Happy Feet*
10) *Bringing Down the House*

Quiz 8

1) "Justice is blind. So is he," is the tagline for what superhero movie?
2) For what cop film did Denzel Washington win his second Best Actor Oscar?
3) *The Blind Side* is based on the true story of a family that takes in a homeless African American teen and helps him succeed in school and become an NFL first round draft pick; what is the name of the player?
4) What Oscar winner provides the voice for Master Shifu in *Kung Fu Panda*?
5) What movie has disgruntled Korean War veteran Walt Kowalski setting out to reform his neighbor, a Hmong teenager?
6) What movie is based on the true story of a rogue wave that hit the *Andrea Gail* fishing boat in the North Atlantic in 1991?
7) What Nicolas Cage and Tea Leoni film has the tagline "What if you made different choices? What if you said yes, instead of no? What if you got a second chance?"
8) "The last man on earth is not alone," is a tagline for what Will Smith movie?
9) In what comedy does an accident cause a chauvinistic executive to hear what women are thinking?
10) What sports-based movie with Keira Knightley in one of her early feature film roles has the tagline "Sometimes, to follow your dreams... you've got to bend the rules!"?

Quiz 8 Answers

1) *Daredevil*
2) *Training Day*
3) Michael Oher
4) Dustin Hoffman

5) *Gran Torino*
6) *The Perfect Storm*
7) *The Family Man*
8) *I Am Legend*
9) *What Women Want* – starring Mel Gibson
10) *Bend It Like Beckham*

Quiz 9

1) In *The Proposal* starring Sandra Bullock and Ryan Reynolds, a pushy boss forces her assistant to marry her to keep her visa; in what city does most of the story take place?

2) What crime drama stars Michael Douglas, Catherine Zeta-Jones, and Benicio Del Toro in a Best Supporting Actor Oscar winning performance?

3) James works at a local amusement park, so he can go to college next year. He falls in love with Emily and learns some life lessons. What is the Jesse Eisenberg movie?

4) Who plays the title role in *Ella Enchanted*?

5) In what movie does Hugh Grant play the role of the British Prime Minister?

6) What movie was filmed entirely in the director's house on a $15,000 budget with a home digital camera and grossed almost $200 million worldwide?

7) What sports comedy features the characters Chazz Michael Michaels and Jimmy MacElroy?

8) In *The Bourne Identity*, the name Bourne comes from Ansel Bourne, a preacher in Rhode Island in the 19th century, who was the first documented case of what mental condition?

9) In the comedy *Nurse Betty*, a woman becomes delusional after her husband's murder and believes she is a nurse in a soap opera; who plays the title role?

10) Who plays the elf Arwen who is Aragorn's love in *The Lord of the Rings: The Return of the King*?

Quiz 9 Answers

1) Sitka, Alaska
2) *Traffic*
3) *Adventureland*
4) Anne Hathaway

5) *Love Actually*
6) *Paranormal Activity*
7) *Blades of Glory*
8) Dissociative fugue - An individual cannot recall some or all of their past. Either the loss of one's identity or the formation of a new identity may occur with sudden, unexpected, purposeful travel away from home.
9) Renee Zellweger
10) Liv Tyler

Quiz 10

1) Who plays the title role in *Bulletproof Monk*?
2) "He finally met the girl of his dreams. Too bad her dad's a nightmare," is the tagline for what Ben Stiller comedy?
3) What Ridley Scott war drama is based on a best-selling book detailing a near-disastrous mission in Somalia on October 3, 1993?
4) What movie tells the story of Captain Jack Aubrey and his crew who are in the pursuit of a French war vessel during the Napoleonic Wars?
5) Who directed *The Lord of the Rings* trilogy?
6) What film is set in Australia in 1931 and features three young mixed-race Aboriginal girls who escape from a government center where they have been sent to be trained as domestic staff and walk 1,500 miles through the Outback to get home?
7) In *Moulin Rouge!*, who plays Toulouse-Lautrec?
8) In what city is the *Twilight* series of movies set?
9) In *WALL-E*, what does WALL-E stand for?
10) In *Ratatouille*, who provides the voice for the food critic Anton Ego?

Quiz 10 Answers

1) *Yun-Fat Chow*
2) *Meet the Parents*
3) *Black Hawk Down*
4) *Master and Commander: The Far Side of the World* – starring Russell Crowe
5) Peter Jackson
6) *Rabbit-Proof Fence*
7) John Leguizamo
8) Forks, Washington – Stephenie Meyer, the author of the books, chose the city because it has the most rainfall in the contiguous 48 states and is small, out of the way, and surrounded by forest.

9) Waste Allocation Load Lifter: Earth-Class
10) Peter O'Toole

Quiz 11

1) In *Shrek*, who provides the voice for the evil Lord Farquaad?
2) Who plays the young woman Bill Murray bonds with in *Lost in Translation*?
3) In *Seabiscuit*, how did Charles S. Howard, Seabiscuit's owner, make his money?
4) In *Ice Age*, Manny, Sid, and Diego are the three heroes who save the human baby; what three kinds of animals are they?
5) In *We Are Marshall*, a plane crash claims the lives of most of the Marshall University football team; what state is Marshall University in?
6) What controversial director won a Best Director Oscar for *The Pianist*?
7) Who plays the Green Goblin in *Spider-Man*?
8) What Guy Ritchie film has unscrupulous boxing promoters, violent bookmakers, a Russian gangster, incompetent amateur robbers, and Jewish jewelers fighting to track down a priceless stolen diamond?
9) In *The Lord of the Rings: The Fellowship of the Ring*, how many are in the original fellowship?
10) Who directed *Mystic River* about three childhood friends whose lives are shattered when one of their daughters is murdered?

Quiz 11 Answers

1) John Lithgow
2) Scarlett Johansson
3) Car dealer
4) Woolly mammoth, sloth, saber-toothed tiger
5) West Virginia
6) Roman Polanski
7) Willem Dafoe
8) *Snatch*
9) Nine – Frodo, Gandalf, Legolas, Gimli, Aragorn, Boromir, Merry, Pippin, Samwise
10) Clint Eastwood

Quiz 12

1) In *Avatar*, what is the name of the moon that is the setting for the

movie?

2) In *Wild Hogs*, four middle-aged men decide to take a motorcycle road trip and end up in trouble with a motorcycle gang; the four men are played by Tim Allen, John Travolta, Martin Lawrence and who?

3) In *Meet the Fockers*, who plays Bernie and Rozalin Focker?

4) What was the most expensive Hollywood film made in the 2000s?

5) What Kevin James comedy has the tagline "Safety never takes a holiday"?

6) *The Life of David Gale* is about an anti-death-penalty activist who is condemned to death for a murder; who plays the title role?

7) How many Harry Potter movies were released in the 2000s?

8) "He puts the mean in green," is the tagline for what comedy?

9) What 2005 film starring Jack Black and Naomi Watts had been made previously in 1933 and 1976?

10) "Meet Elle Woods. She's a lawyer with a heart of gold...and a mane to match!" is a tagline for what comedy?

Quiz 12 Answers

1) Pandora

2) William H. Macy

3) Dustin Hoffman and Barbra Streisand

4) *Pirates of the Caribbean: At World's End* – $300 million

5) *Paul Blart: Mall Cop*

6) Kevin Spacey

7) Six – all but *Harry Potter and the Deathly Hollows: Part 1* and *Harry Potter and the Deathly Hollows: Part 2*

8) *How the Grinch Stole Christmas*

9) *King Kong*

10) *Legally Blonde*

Quiz 13

1) What is the name of Sherlock Holmes romantic interest in *Sherlock Holmes*?

2) What is the name of the horse that Seabiscuit has a match race with in *Seabiscuit*?

3) In *Ratatouille*, what is the name of the rat who can cook voiced by Patton Oswalt?

4) *The Chronicles of Narnia: The Lion, the Witch and the Wardrobe* is based on the book by what author?

5) *The Passion of the Christ* depicts the last 12 hours in the life of Jesus; the film's dialogue is entirely in Hebrew, Latin, and what language?

6) In *Monsters, Inc.*, what two actors provide the voices for Sulley and Mike?

7) What Robert Altman film takes place in 1932 at an English country house where a weekend shooting party is taking place and a murder occurs?

8) What Jack Black comedy has the tagline "He just landed the gig of his life: 4th grade"?

9) *Erin Brockovich* is based on a true story involving one of the biggest class action lawsuits in American history; what was the company that was the target of the lawsuit?

10) In *Million Dollar Baby*, Frankie has a Gaelic phrase embroidered on the back of Maggie's fight robe and won't tell her what it means. What does the phrase mean as he discloses near the end of the movie?

Quiz 13 Answers

1) Irene Adler
2) War Admiral
3) Remy
4) C.S. Lewis
5) Aramaic
6) John Goodman and Billy Crystal
7) *Gosford Park*
8) *School of Rock*
9) Pacific Gas & Electric
10) My darling; my blood

Quiz 14

1) In *Charlie's Angels*, what actresses play the angels?

2) Who directed the three Pirates of the Caribbean movies made in the 2000s?

3) In *WALL-E*, what film does WALL-E watch continuously on videocassette?

4) In *National Treasure: Book of Secrets*, whose diary is at the center of the story?

5) Who plays the ballet teacher in *Billy Elliot*?

6) In *The Da Vinci Code*, what is the name of the military group that is charged with protecting the descendants of Jesus?

7) *Charlie and the Chocolate Factory* is based on a book by what author?

8) In *The Hangover*, the three men searching for the missing groom are played by Bradley Cooper, Ed Helms, and who?

9) Julia Roberts plays an art history teacher at an all-female college in the 1950s and ends up teaching much more than art in what movie?

10) What film centers on the gathering of the eccentric members of a dysfunctional family and stars Gene Hackman, Ben Stiller, Owen Wilson, Luke Wilson, Gwyneth Paltrow, Danny Glover, Bill Murray and Angelica Houston?

Quiz 14 Answers

1) Drew Barrymore, Lucy Liu, Cameron Diaz
2) Gore Verbinski
3) *Hello, Dolly!*
4) John Wilkes Booth
5) Julie Walters
6) Knights Templar
7) Roald Dahl
8) Zach Galifianakis
9) *Mona Lisa Smile*
10) *The Royal Tenenbaums*

Quiz 15

1) *Catch Me If You Can* is based on the true story of Frank Abagnale Jr. who before his 19th birthday passed millions of dollars of bad checks posing as a pilot, doctor, and prosecutor; Leonardo DiCaprio plays Abagnale. Who plays the FBI agent who hunts him down?

2) In *Underworld*, who plays Viktor, the oldest and strongest of the elder vampires?

3) "Joe Kingman had the perfect game plan to win the championship... but first, he has to tackle one little problem," is a tagline for what movie?

4) What film is based heavily on the career of *The Supremes*?

5) Who plays Captain Barbossa in *Pirates of the Caribbean: The Curse of the Black Pearl*?

6) In *Mamma Mia*, there are three potential fathers of the bride played by Pierce Brosnan, Stellan Skarsgård, and what actor?

7) What movie has the Hoover family trying to get to California so that young daughter Olive can compete in a beauty pageant?

8) Heath Ledger and Jake Gyllenhaal play sheep herders in what film?
9) In *X-Men*, what is Wolverine's real name?
10) In *District 9*, an extraterrestrial race is forced to live in slum-like conditions on Earth; what is the nickname humans use for the aliens?

Quiz 15 Answers

1) Tom Hanks
2) Bill Nighy
3) *The Game Plan* – starring Dwayne Johnson
4) *Dreamgirls*
5) Geoffrey Rush
6) Colin Firth
7) *Little Miss Sunshine*
8) *Brokeback Mountain*
9) Logan
10) The Prawns

Quiz 16

1) Based on a true story, what film stars Helen Mirren and Julie Walters as part of a group of middle-aged Englishwomen who raise money for the local hospital in an unusual way?
2) In *Signs*, Mel Gibson plays a preacher who has lost his faith; crop circles begin to appear on his farm and all over the world leading to an alien encounter. Who wrote and directed *Signs*?
3) In *Avatar*, what is the name of the native humanoids?
4) In *The Santa Clause 2*, what is the first name of Santa's eventual bride?
5) In *Georgia Rule*, Lindsay Lohan plays a troubled young woman sent to live with her grandmother for the summer; who plays the title role of the grandmother?
6) What actor died during the filming of *Gladiator*?
7) In *Memento*, who plays Leonard who can no longer form new memories and is trying to find the murderer of his wife?
8) In the spy spoof thriller *Johnny English*, who plays the title character?
9) Who directed *Crouching Tiger, Hidden Dragon*?
10) In *Finding Nemo*, who provides the voice of Nemo's father Marlin?

Quiz 16 Answers

1) *Calendar Girls* – The women pose nude for a fundraising calendar.

2) M. Night Shyamalan
3) Na'vi
4) Carol
5) Jane Fonda
6) Oliver Reed
7) Guy Pearce
8) Rowan Atkinson
9) Ang Lee
10) Albert Brooks

Quiz 17

1) In *Panic Room*, Jodie Foster plays a recently divorced mother who along with her daughter must hide out in a panic room when thieves break in to their new home; who plays her young daughter and went on to star in a very successful film series six years later?
2) What is the real name of superhero Iron Man?
3) Who are the siblings who wrote and directed the *Matrix* trilogy?
4) In *Daddy Day Care*, who plays the tough director of the Chapman Academy who will stop at nothing to drive her competitors out of business?
5) In what science fiction movie does Kevin Spacey say, "Every being in the universe knows right from wrong, Mark"?
6) What is the name of the giant bird in *Up*?
7) Based on a true story, what movie follows Carl Brashear as he attempts to become the first African American U.S. Navy diver?
8) Peter Dinklage stars as a man born with dwarfism who moves to rural New Jersey to live a life of solitude but ends up making friends anyway; what is the movie?
9) A man can hear a female voice narrating his life in what movie?
10) What was the first Dr. Seuss animated feature film?

Quiz 17 Answers

1) Kristen Stewart – star in the *Twilight* films
2) Anthony Stark
3) Lana Wachowski and Lilly Wachowski
4) Anjelica Huston
5) *K-PAX*
6) Kevin

7) *Men of Honor*
8) *The Station Agent*
9) *Stranger Than Fiction* – starring Will Ferrell
10) *Horton Hears a Who!*

Quiz 18

1) In *Whale Rider*, an 11-year-old girl believes she is destined to be her tribes next chief despite a thousand years of tradition; what country is the movie set in?
2) Who plays the Joker in *The Dark Knight*?
3) In *The Santa Clause 3: The Escape Clause*, who plays Jack Frost?
4) What western stars Kevin Costner, Robert Duvall, and Annette Bening and was also the last non-animated film performance of Michael Jeter?
5) What comedy has the tagline "The guy next door just became the guy upstairs"?
6) What historical drama has Jude Law trying to make his way home from the Civil War and also stars Nicole Kidman and Renee Zellweger in a Best Supporting Actress Oscar role?
7) What was the number one U.S. box office film released in the 2000s?
8) Who plays Will Smith's son in *The Pursuit of Happyness*?
9) "Day 1: Exposure - Day 3: Infection - Day 8: Epidemic - Day 15: Evacuation - Day 20: Devastation," is a tagline for what film?
10) In *O Brother, Where Art Thou?*, what is the name of the singing group formed by the three escaped convicts?

Quiz 18 Answers

1) New Zealand
2) Heath Ledger – He won a posthumous Best Supporting Actor Oscar.
3) Martin Short
4) *Open Range*
5) *Bruce Almighty*
6) *Cold Mountain*
7) *Avatar* – 2009
8) Jaden Smith – his real-life son
9) *28 Days Later...*
10) The Soggy Bottom Boys

2010s

Quiz 1

1) What science fiction film has the tagline "AD 2031: the passengers in the train are the only survivors on Earth"?

2) "Welcome to the urban jungle," is a tagline for what Disney animated film?

3) For what film did Natalie Portman win a Best Actress Oscar?

4) Johnny Depp provides the voice for the title character in the animated *Rango*; what kind of creature is Rango?

5) What was the first non-Disney animated film to gross over $1 billion worldwide?

6) What musical stars Emma Watson, Kevin Kline, Ewan McGregor, Emma Thompson, Ian McKellen, and Stanley Tucci?

7) What best Picture Oscar nominee stars Ralph Fiennes, F. Murray Abraham, Adrien Brody, Willem Dafoe, Jeff Goldblum, Harvey Keitel, Jude Law, Bill Murray, and Edward Norton?

8) What musical stars Hugh Jackman, Russell Crowe, Anne Hathaway, Sacha Baron Cohen, and Helena Bonham Carter?

9) *Lady Bird* follows an artistically inclined 17-year-old girl coming of age during her senior year; what city is it set in?

10) In the James Bond movie *Skyfall*, what is Skyfall?

Quiz 1 Answers

1) *Snowpiercer*

2) *Zootopia*

3) *Black Swan*

4) Chameleon

5) *Minions* – 2015

6) *Beauty and the Beast*

7) *The Grand Budapest Hotel*

8) *Les Miserables*

9) Sacramento, California

10) It is the name of the Bond family estate in Scotland.

Quiz 2

1) In *Thor*, what is the name of the bridge that connects Asgard and

Earth?

2) In *The Hunger Games*, what is the name of the futuristic nation?

3) What WWII drama has the tagline "When 400,000 men couldn't get home, home came for them"?

4) The movie *It* is based on a novel by Stephen King; what is the name of the town in Maine where it is set?

5) What was the first animated film to gross $1 billion worldwide?

6) "The park is open," is a tagline for what sequel?

7) Who directed the remake of *True Grit*?

8) In *The Martian*, what is the name of the manned mission that strands Matt Damon's character on Mars?

9) Based on a *New York Times* bestseller, a boy with facial differences attends a mainstream elementary school for the first time in *Wonder*; what is the first name of the boy?

10) With six Oscar wins, what was the fourth movie in the *Mad Max* series?

Quiz 2 Answers

1) Bifrost
2) Panem
3) *Dunkirk*
4) Derry
5) *Toy Story 3*
6) *Jurassic World*
7) Joel and Ethan Coen
8) *Ares III*
9) Auggie
10) *Mad Max: Fury Road*

Quiz 3

1) What film looks at the relationship between physicist Stephen Hawking and his wife Jane Wilde?

2) What movie has the tagline "You don't get to 500 million friends without making a few enemies"?

3) In Best Picture Oscar winner *The King's Speech*, Colin Firth plays what English king who needed a speech therapist to overcome his stammer?

4) What film broke the record for most Golden Globe wins with seven and was also mistakenly announced as the Best Picture Oscar winner?

5) What organization has replaced the Empire as the main enemy of the Resistance in *Star Wars: The Force Awakens*?

6) In *Black Panther*, what is the name of the fictional African nation where the action takes place?

7) What was the first western for both Denzel Washington and Chris Pratt?

8) For what film, did Jean Dujardin become the first French actor ever to win the Best Actor Oscar?

9) Denzel Washington directed and starred in *Fences* which is based on a Pulitzer Prize winning play by what author?

10) In the animated *Mr. Peabody & Sherman*, Mr. Peabody, a genius dog, and his adopted boy Sherman travel through time; what is the name of their time machine?

Quiz 3 Answers

1) *The Theory of Everything*
2) *The Social Network* – story behind Facebook
3) King George VI
4) *La La Land*
5) First Order
6) Wakanda
7) *The Magnificent Seven*
8) *The Artist*
9) August Wilson
10) WABAC machine

Quiz 4

1) *Saving Mr. Banks* is about Walt Disney's attempts to convince the author of *Mary Poppins* to allow him to create a movie based on the story. Tom Hanks plays Walt Disney; Emma Thompson plays the author; what is her name?

2) What was the first of *The Hobbit* trilogy movies?

3) Trying to find a planet that can sustain life and ensure mankind's survival, what space feature do the astronauts in *Interstellar* leverage?

4) Who provides the voice for the bear Baloo in *The Jungle Book*?

5) What animated film's two main characters are Hiccup and Toothless?

6) Who plays the title role in *Noah*?

7) In the comedy *The Heat*, an uptight FBI Special Agent is paired with a foul-mouthed Boston cop to take down a drug lord; who plays the two central characters?

8) In Tim Burton's comedy *Dark Shadows*, Johnny Depp plays what

vampire?

9) What Leonardo DiCaprio film has the tagline "Your mind is the scene of the crime"?

10) Who provides the voice of Dracula in *Hotel Transylvania*?

Quiz 4 Answers

1) P.L. Travers
2) *The Hobbit: An Unexpected Journey*
3) Wormhole
4) Bill Murray
5) *How to Train Your Dragon*
6) Russell Crowe
7) Sandra Bullock and Melissa McCarthy
8) Barnabas Collins – The movie is based on the television soap opera that ran from 1966–1971.
9) *Inception*
10) Adam Sandler

Quiz 5

1) *Magic Mike* is about a group of male strippers; who plays the title role?
2) The true story of the first American cargo ship hijacking in 200 years is the subject of what film?
3) *Alice in Wonderland* is based on a novel by what author?
4) What film stars Bruce Dern and Will Forte as a father and son on a road trip to claim a sweepstakes prize?
5) Who directed *Alice in Wonderland*?
6) Dwayne Johnson, Karen Gillan, Jack Black and what other actor play the four adult versions of the teenagers drawn into the game in *Jumanji: Welcome to the Jungle*?
7) Who plays the title role in *Cinderella*?
8) In *Winter's Bone*, a 17-year-old Ozark Mountain girl looks for her drug-dealing father while trying to keep her family intact; who plays the girl?
9) In *Now You See Me*, the four illusionists are played by Isla Fisher, Dave Franco, Jesse Eisenberg, and what actor?
10) In *Her*, Joaquin Phoenix plays a lonely writer who falls in love with an operating system. Who provides the voice of Samantha, the operating system?

Quiz 5 Answers

1) Channing Tatum
2) *Captain Phillips*
3) Lewis Carroll – pen name of Charles L. Dodgson
4) *Nebraska*
5) Tim Burton
6) Kevin Hart
7) Lily James
8) Jennifer Lawrence
9) Woody Harrelson
10) Scarlett Johannson

Quiz 6

1) What film was shot over 12 years with the same cast and depicts the life of Mason from early childhood to his arrival at college?
2) In *Edge of Tomorrow*, Tom Cruise plays a soldier fighting aliens who lives the same day repeatedly with each day restarting every time he dies; what is the name of the alien race he is battling?
3) Who directed *The Shape of Water*?
4) Who plays the title role in *Doctor Strange*?
5) Based on a true story, *Moneyball* features Billy Beane's success assembling a baseball team on a small budget using statistical data to analyze players; what was the team?
6) Who provides the voice of Groot in *Guardians of the Galaxy*?
7) What animated film has the tagline "An unforgettable journey she probably won't remember"?
8) A mountain climber becomes trapped under a boulder and resorts to desperate measures to survive; what is the movie?
9) What film has Leonardo DiCaprio as a U.S. Marshal who investigates the disappearance of a murderer who escaped from a hospital for the criminally insane?
10) *Argo* is based on a true story about an unusual plan to rescue Americans from what country?

Quiz 6 Answers

1) *Boyhood*
2) Mimics
3) Guillermo del Toro

4) Benedict Cumberbatch
5) Oakland Athletics
6) Vin Diesel
7) *Finding Dory*
8) *127 Hours*
9) *Shutter Island*
10) Iran

Quiz 7

1) What Disney animated feature is based on the fairy tale Rapunzel?
2) "For ten years one woman never stopped searching for the most wanted man in history," is the tagline for what movie?
3) In the animated *Home*, who provides the voice of Oh, an alien on the run from his own people who makes friends with a girl?
4) In *Three Billboards Outside Ebbing, Missouri*, a mother challenges the local authorities to solve her daughter's murder; who won a Best Actress Oscar for her portrayal of the mother?
5) What J.J. Abrams film occurs during the summer of 1979 when a group of friends witness a train crash and investigate subsequent unexplained events in their small town?
6) "Ever wonder what your pets do when you're not home?" is a tagline for what animated film?
7) The *Hunger Games* trilogy is based on whose novels?
8) Joel and Ethan Coen were screenwriters for *Unbroken* which is the story of Olympian Louis Zamperini who survives a plane crash in WWII and spends 47 days in a raft before he's caught by the Japanese and sent to a prisoner of war camp. What actress directed the movie?
9) Matthew McConaughey won the Best Actor Oscar and Jared Leto won the Best Supporting Actor Oscar for what film?
10) *Jurassic World: Fallen Kingdom* is what number film in the *Jurassic Park* series?

Quiz 7 Answers

1) *Tangled*
2) *Zero Dark Thirty* – the hunt for Osama bin Laden
3) Jim Parsons
4) Frances McDormand
5) *Super 8*
6) *The Secret Life of Pets*

7) Suzanne Collins
8) Angelina Jolie
9) *Dallas Buyers Club*
10) Five – *Jurassic Park* (1993), *The Lost World: Jurassic Park* (1997), *Jurassic Park III* (2001), *Jurassic World* (2015), *Jurassic World: Fallen Kingdom* (2018)

Quiz 8

1) What 2010 action film stars Sylvester Stallone, Jason Statham, Dolph Lundgren, Mickey Rourke, Jet Li, Bruce Willis, and Arnold Schwarzenegger?
2) *The Help* is based on a very popular novel that spent more than 100 weeks on the New York Times Best Seller list; who is the author?
3) What Martin Scorsese film is based on the true story of stockbroker Jordan Belfort?
4) A soldier wakes up in someone else's body and discovers he is part of an experimental government program to find the bomber of a commuter train, and he only has eight minutes to complete his mission; what is the movie?
5) "Explore a new era of the wizarding world before Harry Potter." Is a tagline for what movie?
6) Who provides the voice for the title character in Dr. Seuss' *The Lorax*?
7) What western starring Daniel Craig has the tagline "First contact. Last stand"?
8) The story of Jackie Robinson becoming the first modern African American Major League Baseball player is depicted in the movie 42; what is the team that originally signed Robinson?
9) In the animated comedy *Rio*, what kind of birds are Blu and Jewel voiced by Jesse Eisenberg and Anne Hathaway?
10) In *Incredibles 2*, what is the name of the superhero family?

Quiz 8 Answers

1) *The Expendables*
2) Kathryn Stockett
3) *The Wolf of Wall Street*
4) *Source Code*
5) *Fantastic Beasts and Where to Find Them*
6) Danny DeVito
7) *Cowboys & Aliens*
8) Brooklyn Dodgers

9) Macaws
10) Parr

Quiz 9

1) Tom Cruise plays the title role in *Jack Reacher* about a former U.S. Army Military Police officer who investigates a sniper shooting that killed five people; the movie is based on a book by what author?
2) What Best Picture Oscar winner depicts the childhood, adolescence and young adulthood of an African American gay man growing up in a rough Miami neighborhood?
3) Bradley Cooper stars in the biographical war drama *American Sniper* where he plays the deadliest sniper in U.S. military history; who does he portray?
4) In *The Maze Runner*, what are the creatures that live in the maze and attack the Gladers called?
5) What movie has the tagline "The average person uses 10% of their brain capacity. Imagine what she could do with 100%"?
6) In the remake *The Karate Kid*, Jackie Chan plays the kung fu master; who plays the title role?
7) What was the first Best Picture Oscar winner that was shot entirely digitally and was the first winner to have parentheses in the title?
8) What film is about a group of investors who bet against the U.S. mortgage market before the 2008 housing crisis?
9) In *The Descendants*, George Clooney stars as Matt King whose family owns a very large piece of undeveloped land on what island?
10) Leonardo DiCaprio plays the title role in *The Great Gatsby*; what is Gatsby's first name?

Quiz 9 Answers

1) Lee Child
2) *Moonlight*
3) Chris Kyle
4) Grievers
5) *Lucy*
6) Jaden Smith
7) *Birdman or (The Unexpected Virtue of Ignorance)*
8) *The Big Short*
9) Kauai – Hawaii
10) Jay

Quiz 10

1) In *Arrival*, a linguistics professor is recruited by the military to communicate with alien lifeforms after spaceships land in 12 locations around the world; who plays the linguistics professor?
2) What film features the tales of Cinderella, Little Red Riding Hood, Jack and the Beanstalk, and Rapunzel tied together in a single story in a musical format?
3) In *Sing*, who provides the voice of theater owner Buster Moon who creates the singing competition?
4) In *The Fighter*, Mark Wahlberg plays a real-life boxer who went on to become a world champion; who is the boxer?
5) "One of the greatest heroes in American history never fired a bullet," is a tagline for what WWII movie directed by Mel Gibson?
6) Ed O'Neill voices what kind of creature in *Finding Dory*?
7) Denzel Washington plays the title character of a former intelligence agent in *The Equalizer*; what is the character's name?
8) In *Minions*, Sandra Bullock provides the voice for the world's first female supervillain; what is her name?
9) What fantasy film features the character Hushpuppy played by Quvenzhane Wallis who received a Best Actress Oscar nomination?
10) In *Guardians of the Galaxy*, who is Peter Quill's ship named after?

Quiz 10 Answers

1) Amy Adams
2) *Into the Woods*
3) Matthew McConaughey
4) Micky Ward
5) *Hacksaw Ridge* – It is the true story of Desmond T. Doss who as a conscientious objector was awarded the Congressional Medal of Honor for his bravery as a medic.
6) Octopus
7) Robert McCall
8) Scarlet Overkill
9) *Beasts of the Southern Wild*
10) Alyssa Milano – Peter Quill's childhood crush

Quiz 11

1) In Disney's animated *Frozen*, who provides the voice for the central

character Anna?

2) Disney's animated *Brave* featuring Princess Merida is set in what country?

3) What actor and actress play the bored married couple who try to have a glamorous and romantic evening in New York which turns into something more dangerous in the comedy *Date Night*?

4) What movie focuses on three African American female mathematicians and has the tagline "Meet the women you don't know, behind the mission you do"?

5) In *Extremely Loud & Incredibly Close*, nine-year-old Oskar is trying to cope with the death of his father played by Tom Hanks; how did his father die?

6) What is the first film by a black director to win the Best Picture Oscar?

7) In *World War Z*, who plays the former United Nations employee who traverses the world in a race against time to stop the zombie pandemic?

8) What Steven Spielberg drama deals with a freedom of the press fight related to the Pentagon Papers?

9) "The untold story behind the miracle on the Hudson" is a tagline for what movie?

10) What was the first animated feature film produced by Industrial Light & Magic?

Quiz 11 Answers

1) Kristen Bell
2) Scotland
3) Steve Carell and Tina Fey
4) *Hidden Figures*
5) World Trade Center attack
6) *12 Years a Slave*
7) Brad Pitt
8) *The Post*
9) *Sully*
10) *Rango* – 2011

Quiz 12

1) What is the shortest *Harry Potter* movie?
2) What film had 10 Oscar nominations with no wins including acting nominations for Christian Bale, Amy Adams, Bradley Cooper, and Jennifer Lawrence?

3) Based on a true story, Jack Black plays a mortician who befriends and then kills a wealthy widow played by Shirley MacLaine in what movie?

4) *Selma* chronicles the 1965 campaign by Dr. Martin Luther King Jr. to secure equal voting rights via an epic march from Selma, Alabama to what city?

5) Best Picture Oscar winner *Spotlight* tells the true story of a team of investigative journalists that uncover a massive child molestation scandal and cover-up in the Catholic church; what paper do the journalists work for?

6) What Woody Allen film features a nostalgic screenwriter who finds himself mysteriously going back in time to 1920s Paris?

7) What film received Oscar nominations in all four acting categories for Bradley Cooper, Robert De Niro, Jennifer Lawrence, and Jacki Weaver with a win for Jennifer Lawrence?

8) Who won a Best Actor Oscar for their portrayal of Winston Churchill in *Darkest Hour*?

9) Kristen Stewart, Charlize Theron, and Chris Hemsworth star in what classic fairy tale remake?

10) In *Zookeeper*, Kevin James talks to the zoo animals he cares for; who provides the voice for Bernie the gorilla?

Quiz 12 Answers

1) *Harry Potter and the Deathly Hallows: Part 2* – 2 hours and 10 minutes
2) *American Hustle*
3) *Bernie*
4) Montgomery, Alabama
5) Boston Globe
6) *Midnight in Paris*
7) *Silver Linings Playbook*
8) Gary Oldman
9) *Snow White and the Huntsman*
10) Nick Nolte

Quiz 13

1) Seth Rogan plays the title role in *The Green Hornet*; what is the Green Hornet's real name?

2) Who recorded and co-wrote the theme song for *Skyfall* which won a Best Original Song Oscar?

3) Jordan Peele won a Best Original Screenplay Oscar for what horror film

which was also was his directing debut?

4) In the animated *Inside Out*, young Riley is uprooted from her Midwest life and moved to San Francisco, her emotions conflict on how best to adjust to her new life; what five emotions are depicted as characters?

5) A depressed uncle must take over as guardian for his teenage nephew when his brother dies in what film that won Casey Affleck a Best Actor Oscar?

6) What movie set in the 1820s American frontier won Leonardo DiCaprio a Best Actor Oscar?

7) What 2011 film was Martin Scorsese's first PG rated film in 18 years?

8) What Ben Affleck directed film won the Best Picture Oscar?

9) "Help is only 140 million miles away," is the tagline for what movie?

10) In *The Social Network*, what is the name of the website Mark Zuckerberg initially creates to rate the attractiveness of female Harvard students and in the process gets a six-month academic probation?

Quiz 13 Answers

1) Britt Reid
2) Adele
3) *Get Out*
4) Joy, fear, anger, disgust, sadness
5) *Manchester by the Sea*
6) *The Revenant*
7) *Hugo*
8) *Argo*
9) *The Martian*
10) FaceMash

Quiz 14

1) *The Imitation Game* is set during WWII and stars Benedict Cumberbatch as what real-life mathematical genius?

2) *This Is the End* has celebrities playing themselves stuck in a house as the Biblical Apocalypse occurs; what celebrity's house are they stuck in?

3) Paul Walker, one of the stars of the *Fast and Furious* movie series, died part way through the filming of which movie?

4) What horror fantasy has the tagline "President by day. Hunter by night"?

5) "What if a pill could make you rich and powerful?" is a tagline for what film?

6) In *Blade Runner 2049*, Ryan Gosling's character discovers a secret that could tear society apart; what is the secret?

7) Who plays Rooster Cogburn in the *True Grit remake*?

8) What movie marks the second time Sylvester Stallone has been nominated for an Oscar for playing Rocky Balboa?

9) *Star Wars: The Last Jedi* is what number film in the *Star Wars* series?

10) What 2013 film won seven Oscars and has the second most wins in history without winning Best Picture?

Quiz 14 Answers

1) Alan Turing
2) James Franco
3) *Furious 7*
4) *Abraham Lincoln: Vampire Hunter*
5) *Limitless*
6) Replicants can reproduce on their own.
7) Jeff Bridges
8) *Creed*
9) Nine
10) *Gravity*

Quiz 15

1) Daniel Craig stars as a journalist searching for a woman missing for 40 years in *The Girl with the Dragon Tattoo*; what country is the movie set in?

2) What Best Animated Feature Oscar winner features a boy who enters the Land of the Dead?

3) What Quentin Tarantino western was nominated for Best Picture and features Christoph Waltz in the longest Best Supporting Actor Oscar winning performance ever?

4) Special Forces operative turned mercenary Wade Wilson is subjected to a rogue experiment that leaves him with new powers; what is the movie?

5) For what film did Daniel Day-Lewis win his third Best Actor Oscar?

6) Who plays the title role in *Wonder Woman*?

7) What Steven Spielberg Cold War drama stars Tom Hanks as a lawyer recruited to defend a Soviet spy and help the CIA exchange the spy for U2 spy plane pilot Francis Gary Powers?

8) A divorced father and his ex-con older brother resort to a desperate

scheme to save their family's ranch in West Texas in what movie?

9) Ben Affleck stars as Nick Dunne who reports his wife missing and eventually becomes a suspect in her murder in what movie?

10) In *Life of Pi*, what is the name of the tiger?

Quiz 15 Answers

1) Sweden
2) *Coco*
3) *Django Unchained*
4) *Deadpool*
5) *Lincoln*
6) Gal Gadot
7) *Bridge of Spies*
8) *Hell or High Water*
9) *Gone Girl*
10) Richard Parker

If you enjoyed this book and learned a little and would like others to enjoy it also, please put out a review or rating. If you scan the QR code below, it will take you directly to the Amazon review and rating page.

Made in the USA
Middletown, DE
13 January 2022

58629104R00104